Coaching Cross Country Successfully

Pat Tyson

with

Doug Binder

Human Kinetics

Library of Congress Cataloging-in-Publication Data

Library of Congress Cataloging-in-Publication Data
Tyson, Pat, 1950-
    Coaching cross country successfully / Pat Tyson, Doug Binder.
        pages cm
    Includes index.
    1. Cross-country running--Coaching. I. Binder, Doug, 1971- author. II. Title.
    GV1063.2.C62T97 2013
    796.42'8--dc23

                                    2013017613

ISBN-10: 1-4504-4019-3 (print)
ISBN-13: 978-1-4504-4019-6 (print)

The web addresses cited in this text were current as of May 2013, unless otherwise noted.

Acquisitions Editor: Tom Heine; **Developmental Editors:** Claire Marty and Tom Hanlon; **Assistant Editor:** Tyler M. Wolpert; **Copyeditor:** Annette Pierce; **Indexer:** Laurel Plotzke; **Graphic Designer:** Nancy Rasmus; **Graphic Artist:** Yvonne Griffith; **Cover Designer:** Keith Blomberg; **Photograph (cover):** Pat Tyson; **Photographs (interior):** © Human Kinetics, unless otherwise noted; **Photo Asset Manager:** Laura Fitch; **Visual Production Assistant:** Joyce Brumfield; **Photo Production Manager:** Jason Allen; **Art Manager:** Kelly Hendren; **Associate Art Manager:** Alan L. Wilborn; **Illustrations:** © Human Kinetics; **Printer:** United Graphics

We thank Lewis and Clark High School in Spokane, Washington, for assistance in providing the location for the photo shoot for this book.

Human Kinetics books are available at special discounts for bulk purchase. Special editions or book excerpts can also be created to specification. For details, contact the Special Sales Manager at Human Kinetics.

Printed in the United States of America   10 9 8 7 6 5 4 3 2 1

The paper in this book is certified under a sustainable forestry program.

Human Kinetics
Website: www.HumanKinetics.com

United States: Human Kinetics
P.O. Box 5076
Champaign, IL 61825-5076
800-747-4457
e-mail: humank@hkusa.com

Canada: Human Kinetics
475 Devonshire Road Unit 100
Windsor, ON N8Y 2L5
800-465-7301 (in Canada only)
e-mail: info@hkcanada.com

Europe: Human Kinetics
107 Bradford Road
Stanningley
Leeds LS28 6AT, United Kingdom
+44 (0) 113 255 5665
e-mail: hk@hkeurope.com

Australia: Human Kinetics
57A Price Avenue
Lower Mitcham, South Australia 5062
08 8372 0999
e-mail: info@hkaustralia.com

New Zealand: Human Kinetics
P.O. Box 80
Torrens Park, South Australia 5062
0800 222 062
e-mail: info@hknewzealand.com

E5804

To all my ex-teammates known as The Men of Oregon. To all the families who took care of me: Bill and Ruth Berwold, Laurel James and boys, Bill and Marcia McChesney, Kent and Sandy Sullivan, Jerry and Mike Delich, Steve and Carla Loughlin, Mike and Jan Aubrey, Roger and Donna James, Grant and Julie Becherini, Wayne and Cindy Davis, Roger and Roxy Cramer, Bryan and June Geissler, and Bill and Marol Dellinger.

To all those who I coached at Morgan, Kellogg, Shorecrest, Mead, South Eugene, University of Oregon, University of Kentucky, and all my runners at Gonzaga University. You truly are my family.

Pat Tyson

To my daughter, Lily. May you one day be inspired by great teachers such as my friend, Pat Tyson.

Doug Binder

CONTENTS

FOREWORD

Simply put, Pat Tyson was one of the greatest high school cross country coaches ever. In my mind, he's one of the top two, along with Joe Newton from York High in Illinois.

Pat's kids at Mead genuinely loved him and bought into what he was doing. He empowered them to go out and work hard, train correctly, and enjoy running. He guided them without really pushing them.

In cross country, you often find kids who lack confidence in their ability to be athletes. They're not big and strong like the football players, so they tend to come into high school not sure of their place in sports. It's easy for them to not stay with it. But a guy like Pat Tyson gets a kid to come out to practice and give it a try. And ordinarily, those kids might not come back. But they become endeared to Pat. They stick with it because of him.

Pat was never this great athlete at Oregon. Runners like Joaquim Cruz, Rudy Chapa, Bill McChesney, me, and Steve Prefontaine were the names that the running public knew from the University of Oregon. They didn't necessarily know Pat's name, but I can tell you that, within that Oregon family, we not only know Pat but also respect him. What he has done with his life, and in coaching, is perpetuate the Oregon tradition and program more than any other runner, with the possible exception of Pre.

Tyson's formula is a great model for high school coaches to follow because it's filled with positive energy that reaches kids and has valuable information about the right way to train and develop a love for running.

Alberto Salazar
Coach of the Nike Oregon Project
and 2012 Olympic medal winners
Mo Farah and Galen Rupp

PREFACE

Even though I coach at Gonzaga University now, many people across the country will always think of me as a high school cross country coach first, and I'm OK with that.

I started coaching 40 years ago at Morgan and Kellogg Junior High Schools in suburban Seattle and was content to stay there for ten years before taking my first high school job. I was blessed to spend three years at Shorecrest High School and 20 at Spokane's Mead High School. I was fortunate to have the athletes and support and resources to win 14 Washington state boys cross country championships.

It is the work that went into building the program at Mead that is reflected in *Coaching Cross Country Successfully*, and it is my sincere hope that the information contained in these pages is a go-to reference guide for any high school cross country coach.

I must tip my cap to legendary coach Joe Newton of York High School in Illinois, who wrote the first *Coaching Cross Country Successfully*. That book established the template and guided the organization of this book. Joe Newton's book offered one way of doing things. This book tells the tale from a different perspective, reflecting my personality, my high-energy approach to coaching, and my outside-the-box thinking and problem solving.

With the help of one of my friends, writer Doug Binder, who covered track at *The Oregonian* and was an editor for DyeStat, I have tried to articulate all of the pieces that go into building a running culture in a high school.

The information that is gathered here didn't all come out of my brain. My coaching career was built on what I learned from what I call "the voices in my life." Those include my own high school coach, Dan Watson of Lincoln High in Tacoma, Washington, and University of Oregon stalwarts Bill Bowerman and Bill Dellinger. Also, I owe something to Steve Prefontaine for showing me the mental and physical approaches that he took on the way to becoming the best American distance runner of his day.

The culture has shifted over the past 15 years, with high school kids more and more attached to their cell phones and video games than ever before. While cross country participation remains high across the country, I believe that it's getting harder to win kids' attention and convince them to work their entire bodies instead of only their thumbs.

That's why we need more cross country coaches who are Pied Pipers, go-getters who attract and recruit through high energy and creating buzz. No matter what else changes with technology and its increasing ability to distract us and make us sedentary, kids still want to make connections with each other and take part in a group effort that feels rewarding.

Coaching Cross Country Successfully is a blueprint for using distance running as a way to build a hard-working club that is committed to reaching its common goals. We begin by exploring our roots and coming up with an overriding philosophy and then determining how to communicate that approach to attract prospective runners and keep them interested. We delve into one of my favorite aspects of coaching, which is motivation, and explore the techniques that I used to keep cross country fun and cool in the eyes of the athletes.

Then we take a close look at the nuts and bolts of cross country training. Using one of my final seasons at Mead as an example, I have broken down the fall training schedule into a day-by-day accounting of how each workout and each team function fits together. I also include strength and core drills, stretching, and fitness exercises that are designed to make your young athletes faster, stronger, and healthier.

We then examine racing, how to rehearse for competition day, and how to use organization and readiness to prepare for success. Also, I explain what goes into race-day motivation, from shadowing excellence to arriving at the starting line with a killer attitude.

I have delivered these messages in pieces over and over at clinics and camps across the country, but in *Coaching Cross Country Successfully* I have assembled all of the pieces into one cohesive book.

I believe that kids run best when they feel frisky and free to explore their own limits, and I have held onto that notion ever since my association with Prefontaine. It is my hope that the things that I learned from him will also inform your coaching, and that the fire that burned inside of Pre will ignite something in your kids as it did for runners at Mead.

Pat Tyson

ACKNOWLEDGMENTS

To my mother, Alice, a widow since I was seven, who laid down very few rules and let me be a kid. (She never said no.) We didn't have many material possessions, but she always had breakfast, lunch, and dinner ready and a wonderful loving attitude about life. She was my best friend.

To Jim Berwold and Sam Ring, my two best friends growing up in my South Tacoma neighborhood. They were great running buddies who would become high school track and cross country coaches. They are still two of my best buddies.

To Dan Watson, my coach at Lincoln High School, who believed in me and encouraged me to go to the University of Oregon and who impacted my life forever. He was a tremendous father figure.

To my college coach, Bill Dellinger, who never gave up on me even as I struggled as a walk-on athlete at the University of Oregon. Bill also became a father figure who, to this day, is one of my best friends. The workouts he gave me are timeless.

To Bill Bowerman, the head track coach at the University of Oregon, who taught me many lessons about life, including that, by working hard, believing in yourself, and never giving up, you always have a chance.

To Steve Prefontaine, my college teammate, roommate, and best friend. He taught me how to relax and have fun as a runner and mentored me to believe in myself and my potential.

To Doris Brown Heritage, five-time world cross country champion, who has always supported the teams I've coached over the years.

To Loren Saxby (Morgan Junior High), Arnie Johannesen (Kellogg Junior High), Chuck Taylor (Shorecrest High School), Steve Hogue (Mead High School), and Mick Miller (Mead High School). They were my building principals who never said no to any of my requests as a teacher and coach. They let me be me!

To all the coaches who have influenced me throughout my coaching career: Tracy Walters, Herm Caviness, Mike Hadway, Harry Johnson, Bob Barbero, Brock Hogel, Jon Knight, Walt Lange, Joe Newton, Bob Larson, Patty Ley, Jerry Sullivan, Sam Ring, Tom Rothenberger, Bill Brist, Steve Kiesel, Rich Nelson, Forest Braden, Joe Vigil, Don Webber, and Vin Lananna.

And finally, Geoff Hollister, head of Nike Grass Roots Running, who I could always count on for advice on coaching and life and his posse Johnny Truax, Josh Rowe, Alberto Salazar, Rudy Chapa, John Capriotti, Tony Bignell, Tom Redding, Chris Cook and Nelson Farris who gave inspiration to our teams over the years. Geoff specifically had this philosophy: It's not about how long you live but how you contribute. It's about doing your best and doing the right thing. It's about recovering from your mistakes and not giving up. It's about the baton pass to the new generation. It's about the realization that you cannot go it alone. It takes a team.

Pat Tyson

Growing up in Oregon and learning about the sport of track and field in general, and distance running in particular, I idolized Steve Prefontaine. So simply getting to know Pat Tyson and seeing his charisma and his caring attitude has been an honor. Thank you to all of my colleagues who have extended friendship and inspired me and helped me find a way to write about track and field for a living: Ken Goe and Curtis Anderson, Jim McDannald, John and Donna Dye, Steve Underwood, Dave Devine, Jack Pfeifer, Dr. Norbert Sander, and Ross Krempley. To all of the athletes and coaches I have had the pleasure to write about over the years, thank you for your patience and the time you have taken to tell me your stories.

Doug Binder

PART I

COACHING FOUNDATION

Developing a Coaching Philosophy

In every corner of the United States, cross country has a heartbeat maintained by a community of participants, coaches, parents, and followers. It is fall season team running, and year after year its schedule is welded onto the calendar from August to November the same way high school football is. Cross country doesn't scream for attention the way football does, and it's always been that way. Long-distance running is a deeply personal experience. It asks each person for effort, commitment, and determination. And the rewards aren't free. Each runner has to hurt sometimes in order to get ahead. Cross country is a team sport in which success is measured by the collective willingness to hurt for one another, to push for one another, and to become part of something larger.

Just because cross country doesn't often produce the same local media coverage as football, our sport is no less evolved. Over the past 10 to 15 years, cross country's many small thriving pockets have found one another on the Internet. The Foot Locker Cross Country Championships is into its fourth decade celebrating the cream of the crop among American high school runners. And Nike Cross Nationals has altered the landscape, too. Tradition-laden programs and supremely talented individuals from all across the United States now have the chance to find out how they measure up against runners from other states. Media coverage of the larger national community, statistics and results, and training information have never been more present or available to fans passionate enough to follow it.

Building a successful program is what this book is about, and the process doesn't happen overnight. Behind every state championship program and every elite individual, there is a great deal of planning, commitment, and work that has been done behind the scenes. It is a day-by-day, season-by-season endeavor.

When you drive past a beautiful house, the first things you notice are parts of the exterior—the windows, the roof, the landscaping. But none of those things goes into place until a sturdy foundation is in place. So that's where we're going to start, with strategies for laying the cornerstones.

Courtesy of Price Photography

Cross country is a rite of fall at high schools all across the United States and in some places, like Spokane, Washington, the tradition of success spans decades.

My philosophy is based on building a rich tradition of excellence. I follow the deep roots of my masters: Dan Watson (Lincoln High School in Tacoma), Bill Bowerman (University of Oregon), and Bill Dellinger (University of Oregon). What I've learned from them is what it takes to be a champion, and it is almost too easy: hard, consistent work! Running every day! As my three coaches told me, "You've got to love to run." So, they taught me to love running. You also have to train smart. I've learned how a collection of workouts can move runners toward their best performances.

From my mentors, my coaching philosophy has always been to give your best, dream big, and take risks. Remember the power of the rich tradition laid down from runners of the past.

Pat Tyson
Mead High School Head Coach

Tap Into Tradition

Welcome to Spokane, Washington. On the face of it, there doesn't appear to be anything exceptional about this midsize city of 210,000 people. It is an out-of-the-way place permeated by a blue-collar work ethic and an underdog's hunger for recognition.

In the world of running, it is much more. Spokane has been called the Rift Valley of the United States, a tagline meant to associate the area with the highlands of Kenya where many of the world's best distance runners are born and grow up. Ever since the early 1960s, Spokane has produced a long line of exceptional runners, including legends like Gerry Lindgren and Rick Riley, and schools that seem to never run out of great coaching and excellent runners. Cross country is not only fashionable in Spokane, it's also cool. It's part of the identity. The annual Lilac Bloomsday Run, a 12K road race held each May, draws 45,000 to 60,000 participants every year. It's the biggest civic event in the city.

The Greater Spokane League—with schools like Rogers, Shadle Park, Ferris, North Central, and Mead—has dominated Washington state in cross country for decades and is aptly recognized as the best conference in America when it comes to high school long-distance running. At Rogers, Tracy Walters was an exceptional coach and influential figure in Spokane since his days as Lindgren's high school coach. At Ferris, Tony Dolphin and Herm Caviness (who groomed Riley for the U.S. high school two-mile [3,200 m] record) were a formidable coaching team. They passed the torch to Mike Hadway, who raised the intensity level even higher. Shadle Park had longtime coach Vern Page, another running guru. And at North Central there was Len Long, one of Lindgren's former

The Spokane Coaching Tree

Every high school in Spokane owns valuable pieces of the city's rich tradition in distance running. Over decades, these schools may be up or down, but all of them have contributed something memorable to the big picture. All of today's athletes run in the footprints of legends and tell tales of championships that are passed from one generation of coaches and runners to the next.

Here is a closer look at the tradition of some of the high schools in the Greater Spokane League:

- **Rogers:** Tracy Walters is the godfather of distance coaching in Spokane running lore and was the head coach at Rogers from 1956 to 1966. His teams won state titles in 1963 and 1965, but it was his star, Gerry Lindgren, who was a mythic local hero. Lindgren competed in the Olympic Games 10,000 meters in 1964 while still in high school.

- **Shadle Park:** The Highlanders won the very first Washington state boys cross country championship in 1959 and won the team title again in 1962. Later, Vern Page took the helm and led Shadle Park to the 1982 championship. He was an effective motivator, and his teams regularly fielded more than 100 runners, which helped move the needle for the entire GSL. The school recently produced 2010 state champ Nathan Weitz, who was third at the Foot Locker national championship in 2011.

- **North Central:** Len Long was a high school teammate of Gerry Lindgren and was coached by Walters and led North Central to the 1977 state championship during his time as head coach (1968-86). Starting in the early 1990s, Spokane native Jon Knight took the helm and built a state and national power with Long as his trusted assistant. North Central

won seven Class 3A titles in a row through 2012. North Central won Nike Cross Nationals in 2007 and was third in 2012. Knight's daughter, Katie, was the 2011 state champion and one of the top runners in the country.

- **Ferris:** Tony Dolphin was the first cross country coach for the Saxons when the school opened in the fall of 1963, and he coached the great Rick Riley (8:48 national high school two-mile record) to an individual state title in 1965 and earned a team championship in 1968. Herm Caviness coached Ferris distance runners in track from the school's origins in the spring of 1964 and was the school's head cross country coach from 1969 to 1982. He led Ferris to titles in 1980 and 1981. Mike Hadway took over the distance runners in the 1990s and coached five state-title teams from 2003 to 2009. Ferris was second at the 2009 Nike Cross Nationals.

- **University:** Bob Barbero was the distance running coach at University from 1977 to 1999, winning state three times in a row before stepping down.

- **Central Valley:** Coach Kieran Mahoney student taught under me at Mead High School and was a volunteer coach during that time. In his third year guiding Central Valley, the Bears won their first Washington 4A team championship in the fall of 2012.

- **Mead:** In 1959, Frank Knott was the first individual state champion. Duane Hartman coached the Panthers to the 1976 state championship. I coached at Mead from 1986 to 2005, and we were fortunate to win 12 state team titles. Recent standout Andrew Gardner (class of 2013) competed in three Foot Locker national finals.

high school teammates. University had Bob Barbero. These guys all knew their stuff and collectively drove the well-earned reputation of the GSL.

When I became the cross country coach at Mead in 1986, I knew what I was stepping into. I had always known Mead had a special ring to it. It's one syllable, a powerful-sounding word, and it's in the Greater Spokane League, which is competitive. After 13 years in the Seattle area, on the west side of the state, I knew that there would be pressure to succeed at Mead and that the other coaches in Spokane had set the bar very high. I also saw a sleeping giant, a large school with a mix of upper-class suburban families and working-class families. And it was surrounded by great places to run. The area was close to trails and bike paths, quiet neighborhood sidewalks, grassy fields, hills, and even a shallow river. I am a strong proponent of finding places to run that aren't boring.

I was also holding an ace up my sleeve. I was convinced that the Oregon system, as I'd learned it in college, would be the engine that would drive the program to new heights.

Origins as a Runner

I also thought I had something to bring to the table as a coach. I grew up in Tacoma, Washington, and once I latched onto distance running in high school, I was fortunate to be connected to a rich history. Lindgren and Riley became my idols. My high school coach at Lincoln, Dan Watson, took me to see them race whenever they came close enough for us to drive to see them. I even wrote letters to Riley, a product of Spokane's Ferris High School, while he was at Washington State University. Better yet, he wrote me back and answered all my questions.

Watson also was a big fan of the University of Oregon because his parents lived near Eugene. I felt like I was making him proud when I enrolled at Oregon, where I quickly became immersed in the running culture developed by Bill Bowerman and his assis-

tant, three-time Olympian Bill Dellinger. A year after I started at Oregon, a new high school superstar joined the team: Steve Prefontaine. It took a couple of years—I had to prove myself worthy as a runner first—but I became friends with Pre and we lived together in a trailer park east of campus.

With all of those personalities to learn from and resources to pull from, I developed my own voice as a teacher and coach. I knew that I had come from a rich heritage with so much inspirational material and technical know-how that it steered me into my life's calling.

Not everyone has that same pool of experience to draw on. I was very lucky. But every aspiring coach should be able to locate an authentic tradition or hero or guru that can serve as a starting point for framing a philosophy. If you haven't rubbed shoulders with it like I have, you can still research it. Who is your area's all-time great runner? What coach in your part of the country was the most successful and why? You can find those answers and fold them into what your program stands for. If you still can't find a local tradition to tap into, dig a little deeper until you find one that you can adopt. I'll be glad to share mine with you. If there is something in my story that resonates with you, go ahead and use it!

An Introduction to Pre

It was the summer of 1968 and I was leaning toward making my final decision to attend the University of Oregon. The real clincher was the invitation that Bill Dellinger extended to me to come to Eugene and watch a special pre-Olympic warm-up competition for the U.S. national team before they left for Mexico City.

When I got to Eugene, I went to Bill Dellinger's house for dinner, and he showed me a film of his race at the 1964 Tokyo Olympics. I also found out that I was going to be paired with another prospective student-athlete who was visiting from Coos Bay, Oregon.

Imago/Icon SMI

Distance runner Steve Prefontaine, a 1972 U.S. Olympian, was a source of inspiration in life and remains so many years after his death in 1975.

At that time, I didn't know who Steve Prefontaine was. He was between his junior and senior years of high school. I could tell right away that he had far more confidence than I did. He wore a purple and gold letterman jacket that he was very proud of and he wasn't afraid to talk to college girls who were two to three years older than him. I was impressed.

I sat next to him at the meet and we watched a great distance dual between Oregon's Kenny Moore and Lindgren, my idol from my home state. It was the highlight of the meet. Hayward Field was packed to the rafters, and I had never heard a crowd make so much noise at a track meet before. The place was electric. I was sold that very night, and I believe the high school kid I was sitting next to took notice, too.

Within the next year, the barrel-chested boy from the blue-collar Oregon coastal logging town became a very well-known runner, even breaking Rick Riley's national high school two-mile record (8:41.5).

It's almost unfathomable today to think that two American high school runners could be among the best in the world, but in the early 1960s that was the case. Gerry Lindgren, from Washington, and Jim Ryun, from Kansas, were the faces of U.S. distance running when they were still in high school. Both made the 1964 Olympic team straight out of their senior year.

Everyone tried to emulate those guys. Gerry and Jim were high-mileage guys, and we'd read about their workouts and then want to copy them. We were all catching the wave of high volume. If Lindgren and Ryun were doing it, we all needed to run 70 to 100 miles (113-161 km) per week. Lindgren was probably doing a lot more miles than that, and Ryun's workouts were crazy. The 20 × 400-meter workout that Ryun did, we later turned that into a two-man, 10-mile (16 km) relay. That became a staple when I coached at Mead.

But growing up in Washington state, we looked at Lindgren as one of our own. He showed what was possible if you were willing to work hard enough. He was 5 feet, 6 inches tall (1.7 m) and 120 pounds (54.4 kg), just a little geek from Rogers High School. We all thought, *If he can do it, I can do it!*

Of course, he was also a phenomenon with a talent for running that was almost out of this world. When he ran against the Russians in the 10,000 meters at the Coliseum in Los Angeles, just 18 years old against Soviet Union men in their mid-20s and beat them, he came back to Spokane a hero of the Cold War. His face was on the sports' pages. Lindgren was the one who put Spokane on the map. I got to see him in person a little later, when he was running for Washington State. He ran 12:53 in the three mile and nearly broke the world record in Seattle on a rainy, windy day.

Then came Rick Riley, from Ferris High School in Spokane, two years behind Lindgren. Ferris had a grass track, and that's

> continued

> Gerry Lindgren, Jim Ryun, and Rick Riley *continued*

Gerry Lindgren (right) helped establish the template for what is possible in distance running for anyone willing to work hard enough.

what Riley did his workouts on. As a junior and senior he got crazy good and broke the national record in the two mile with 8:48. What I learned from those guys was how to put together a high-mileage day: You do a morning run and an afternoon run. And then you do a long run on Sundays.

Accentuate the Positive

As you build a philosophy to guide your program, think about where you came from and why you're coaching cross country. It is likely that you were once a high school runner. What were your sources of inspiration? Who taught you, not only how to run but *why* to run? Even if you weren't a runner, you probably wouldn't be coaching unless you had an interest in running. Refer to whatever it is that started you down this path, embrace it, and start building on it. When you know what is inside you that makes you coach and why you love running, that will form the bedrock of your program, what it stands for, and what it is founded on.

Every school has its plusses and minuses. Work to understand and identify your advantages. Does your administration support your program? Can you find volunteers easily? Are there a variety of good places to run? Find the mystique that is particular to your school, whatever it is, and build it up to your athletes. Get them excited to wear the uniform because it means something special.

Some schools have built-in minuses that are difficult to overcome. If you are situated in a school with low socioeconomic factors, an apathetic attitude toward running, a weak tradition, or you get no administrative support, you could easily throw in the towel. Those factors are tough to overcome. The way to attack those deficits is with positive energy, the kind that attracts kids, builds friendships with teaching and coaching peers, and mobilizes parents. Where there is a will there is a way!

Even at Mead High School we had kids in tough situations. One of my top runners was one of those guys. He grew up in a trailer park much like the one Pre and I lived in while we attended the University of Oregon. While this runner had a loving, single mother, he really needed something positive to feed into. I smothered him with the Mead positive energy that I developed in my teams, and he bought into it all—the family of runners, the pizza gatherings, the road trips to new trails, and the idea that running made him a part of something. He evolved into one of the greatest runners in Washington State history when he became the cross country state champion and qualified for the Foot Locker Cross Country Championships.

At Mead, every runner I coached understood that it was an honor to wear those four letters on his chest. Every runner understood the Spokane legacy, and it became a badge of honor when we traveled to meets in other cities. Wherever you are, you can find a kernel of that sort of tradition. You may not have tales of Gerry Lindgren or Steve Prefontaine to rally around, but there is surely something you can latch onto. Kids are attracted to greatness, especially during the high school years when they are maturing and growing and wondering what their limits are.

When I started at Morgan Junior High, I was starting from scratch. I said to myself, "I don't know how we're going to win, but we're going to win." We're going to show up for practice every day and call our perfect attendance a win. We're going to have a great attitude every day and call it a winning attitude. Sometimes winning on the cross country course comes well after you've built a winning program.

To me, a winning program is one that kids want to be part of. They want to be part of it because it's fun, because it's challenging, and because it's competitive. And by win I don't mean literal victories so much as the small accomplishments or achieved goals that mark progress. There is value in taking the time to appreciate and take encouragement from all of them. At the beginning, I knew that our effort might not show right away in the score. But I brought what I learned in high school and college and associated with people who were highly motivated. They were winners. So that became my mission: Promote it and live it, and winning will happen.

Get Them to Love It

I started with the basic premise that my job as a coach was to get kids not only interested in running, but to love it as well. Cross country should feel like an after-school club. It should be the thing that students look forward to all day long until the final classroom bell rings. Coming to cross country practice and into the clubhouse, should be a joy and not feel like a chore. As a coach, your job is to bring an unrelenting supply of positive energy. That's the electrical charge that creates the buzz that makes kids want to join the team. When kids join cross country, they become part of a second family. They want to be loved. They want to be part of something big. They want to feel connected. They want to be noticed.

I used my own experience from high school to guide me. My coach, Dan Watson, used to leave copies of *Track and Field News* around where I could pick them up and read about all

Formulating a Mission Statement

You can begin to develop a foundation by thinking about what constitutes success and what type of program you want to build. What do you stand for? Every program should be guided by a few simple overarching principles.

1. Create an atmosphere that students want to be part of.
2. Bring energy and enthusiasm every day so that the kids are in touch with it daily.
3. Build a sense of family, community, and belonging.
4. Tap into greatness, show it to your runners, and model it.
5. Become part of the tradition that exists locally and identify with it.

of the exciting things happening in the sport. He used to take me to meets on the weekends where I could see firsthand the runners that I idolized. I firmly believe in exposing young athletes to the wider world of track so that they can experience greatness for themselves. I hung posters around my classroom and showed videos of Olympic races to my team. I took the novice and junior varsity teams to the state championships so those kids could see it for themselves.

I didn't have YouTube at my disposal, but if I were coaching at the high school level today, I would absolutely use that site for inspiration. I'd show them Billy Mills winning the 1964 Olympic 10,000 against all odds. I'd show them Prefontaine fighting to take the lead and hold onto it in the 1972 Olympic 5,000 meters. Pre would eventually lose the lead with less than 200 meters remaining and fade to fourth 20 meters before the finish line, but his drive and his focus are inspirational. I'd show them Frank Shorter, Alberto Salazar, Joan Benoit Samuelson, Bob Kennedy, Mary Slaney, Hicham El Guerrouj, Alan Webb, Haile Gebrselassie, Jenny Simpson, Galen Rupp, and anyone else who can show my team what greatness looks like.

Letter From Matt Davis to Mead Cross Country Runners

This is a prestate letter from Matt Davis, who was the Washington 3A cross country champion in 1991, 1992, and 1993 and is the only runner in state history to win the individual title three consecutive years.

Dear Mead Boys:

I want to take a brief moment to encourage you all and possibly give you some words of insight.

If you are nervous: Great! That means you will run awesome. If you are calm: Super! Because you will run awesome as well.

The training's done. The hay's in the barn. Now it's up to each individual to decide before he places a toe on the starting line that *today is my day.* I will run strong and aggressive the first mile. I will attack the second. And destroy the third.

If my opponent has five gears, I have seven. If he wants to push the pace, I will match him. If he digs deep, I will dig deeper. Determine that you will not give up. Believe in the goal of the team and do your best.

Have fun! You have done the work, and you have the best coach. You are the best team!

> Light as a feather
> Strong as a bear
> Fast as a cheetah

> Best of skill,
> Matthew

The family was built by watching videos and dreaming big together, working hard in practice together, and also spending time as a group away from school. Once a week, we met at a local pizza place that I had arranged a deal with. Five bucks got each kid all-you-can-eat pizza and a drink. We showed up every Tuesday evening, sometimes with as many as 50 kids.

Another way to get kids hooked on running is to make everything you can a win. It doesn't matter whether a runner is the best athlete on your team or the worst. All of them can set a personal best. All kids can improve their fitness, lose excess weight, learn healthy habits, and train their bodies to move faster. But you can also go far deeper than that. Find something every day that is positive, highlight it, and create the sense that there is collective momentum building toward something very good. That thing could be a state championship or it could be finishing one spot higher than the previous year at the district finals. Improvement of any kind is progress toward success and fulfillment.

Summary

Developing a coaching philosophy means taking the time to decide just what it is that you stand for, which thoughts and ideas will serve as cornerstones of your instruction, and how you define success.

- Success in the sport of cross country is a byproduct of organization, dedication, and plain old hard work.
- To keep runners engaged and keep them inspired and dreaming, find ways to connect what you do to relevant traditions and legends. Almost every coach has personal experience to call on or has links to a running story from the past that is worthy of talking about and learning from.
- Accentuate the positive. Make the most of the resources that are available in your community and school.
- Do everything you can to make cross country fun. Running is hard work, but kids will put in the effort if they see value in, and reward from, being part of the team and chasing goals.

CHAPTER 2 | Communicating Your Approach

By the time I showed up in Spokane in August of 1986, I had built up my resume by teaching and coaching for 10 years in the Seattle area. I spent four years at Morgan Junior High (1973-77) and six more at Kellogg Middle School (1977-83), and then I took a job at Shorecrest High School (1983-86). My boys at Shorecrest went 26-1 in dual meets and won the school's first state championships in cross country in 1984 and 1985.

When the Mead job came open, I felt that it was too good an opportunity to pass up, so I applied and got the job. The outgoing coach, Tom Buckner, gave me a short list of names and phone numbers so that I could get started by contacting the juniors and seniors on the team.

Legally, we could only hold one preseason meeting, so with the help of one of the seniors, Jeff Rettman, I was able to contact all of the kids and ask them to meet at the school one warm evening. We met on a grassy area near the football field, and I had everyone sit in a circle. There were about 20 boys in the group. (At Mead, I only coached boys. However, all of the information in this book applies equally to girls). They were as nervous as I was. In all early-season meetings there is paperwork, so we talked our way through that.

My mission for that first meeting was to let them know who I was and share my values and goals. I talked about three principles that I picked up from watching football coach Lou Holtz: trust, commitment, caring. After I explained these things to them, I asked each guy to share a competitive goal and what he wanted to accomplish for the good of the team. I promised to give them my best effort and told them that I expected the same from each of them.

I also wanted to make them feel relaxed and comfortable. I told them we'd have weekly pizza gatherings and outings to Dairy Queen for Blizzards. I said we'd work hard and play hard. Again, my goal was to capture them and inspire them. First impressions really do lay the foundation for relationships, and I was eager to leave a strong impression.

When you look kids in the eyes as you talk and listen to them, and when you remember their names, the impact is huge. That first night we played a name game. In this game, one by one, a kid says his or her name out loud. Then you go around the circle and everyone must repeat that person's name. It might seem silly, but name recognition and the ability to learn something about each person goes a long way toward connecting as a group.

By the middle of October, we had put ourselves in a position to go to state, but the competition in the Greater Spokane League was fierce and only two teams would qualify. We were not really in the mix. We lost two dual meets, a close one to Ferris and a convincing defeat to Shadle Park. However, we did upset North Central in the last dual meet of the season and that was a good sign. Rettman, one of our top seniors, had been hurt a lot that season but rejoined the team for the North Central dual. Then at the district meet, we pulled off second place, squeaking into a state championship berth by one point.

I was into Digger Phelps, the basketball coach at Notre Dame, at that time. I had read how the night before Notre Dame beat UCLA to end the Bruins' record 88-game winning streak, Phelps had his players visualize what it would be like to win, even though few people outside the team gave them much of a chance. I loved that idea of overcoming the odds through the intensity of focus and the power of belief.

So I decided to do that, too. I loaded up my first team of Mead guys for the state meet and we went over to the coast side of the state, to Port Townsend, a week before the state meet (700 miles roundtrip). I still had my house near Shorecrest and so we spent the night there and the next morning took the ferry across Puget Sound to the state meet course for a simulation workout. We visualized firing on all cylinders and rehearsed a smashing success for Mead. And then I took them back across the sound to Seattle, and we went to the Space Needle to have dinner and celebrate like we'd already won the championship.

On meet day, my guys finished ninth in the state championship meet. (Shadle Park was 13th). I knew deep down we weren't really ready to win it, but visualizing success helped lay the groundwork for the future. It was a young team, and every one of the guys saw what it would take to be a champion.

Right away, it was apparent that we were building something special at Mead. We did some good workouts that first fall, and the guys had already dialed into the routine of morning runs before school. That tradition had already been established, and I was only too glad to keep it going.

Some of the older kids quickly bought in, like Rettman and Chris Anderson and Robby Parker. They were willing to commit to what I

When a coach shows an interest in each individual by learning names and offering attention, the whole group tends to respond positively.

had laid out for them: shadowing excellence, training year-round, embracing the morning run, taking long runs on Sunday, keeping a journal, and committing to eating and sleeping well. A couple others, Chris Lewis and Rodney Howell, were sophomores who weren't quite there yet. I had to cultivate their interest a bit more. I always made sure kids didn't just show up for practice, but instead were engaged in the process. That's important.

I took Chris Lewis after practice to get French fries or a Big Gulp. I tried to connect with each runner, and after a while they felt loyal to me and the program, and they bought in. Chris loved to get a ride home, and so I would take him. And while we were in the car, I could tell him how good I thought he could be. During cross country season you only have 14 weeks to accomplish your goals, and that first year was supposed to be a building year. In the Greater Spokane League, standings are kept via wins and losses in dual meets and the champion is crowned based on dual meet record. To finish the season 6-2 was way above the curve.

All around Mead were cool places to run. There was a lot of variety, which I emphasized because it kept things fresh and loose. The kids responded when I told them we were keeping things simple, keeping them raw. I was still in pretty good shape and so I ran also, and I could beat all of the guys in workouts. Chris Lewis, as a junior, was the first guy who could beat me. I have always believed it is important to keep the tempo challenging and demonstrate what an advanced level of running looks like, whether it be a long run, interval, or something in between. It also affects your athletes positively when they see you sharing the experience of hard work with them. I'll explain later how this is a role you can hand off to an assistant coach.

In general, I tried to be creative and keep things fun so that I could win the kids over. You almost have to put yourself in their shoes to understand them. They're just coming out of a full day of classes, and the rest of the world views running as punishment. So how did I make it fun?

Creating a Clubhouse Culture

I am a firm believer that you have to have a home base. It may be your classroom. At Mead, I used both my classroom and a small locker room that I inherited from the previous coach. We created a shrine in there with posters, a list of records, photos, inspirational quotes, and anything else that the guys wanted to add.

We had that locker room and maintained it throughout the school year. It was the clubhouse where the guys could meet, do homework, and get dressed to run and then come back and shower. We set it up like it was a club. We had a small refrigerator and a microwave. I collected their towels and washed them. I bought shampoo and soap at a warehouse store and kept them stocked. I think parents liked that. They didn't have to worry about the cost of showers at home. A company gave us 10 racks for hanging wet shoes to dry.

Another important aspect of the clubhouse was music. I made cassettes, recording songs off the radio, and the guys played them on a portable stereo. Of course, today that sounds dated. Now you'd download all your favorite songs and put them on an MP3 player or iPod. But it's the same idea: creating an environment that your team wants to be in.

I've always liked the locker room camaraderie. We put a strip of medical tape on each kid's locker and wrote his last name on it. It was a place for everybody on the team to hang out and enjoy the clubhouse effect. You get the same effect from the morning run. You might wonder about the value of a morning run before school: Does a 20- to 30-minute run really help these guys become better runners or is it important because it's something they do together, that connects them and builds a tight bond? I think those are moments the guys take with them and never forget, just like singing songs in the locker room. You're never going to get that same feeling just by going to the field, doing a workout, and then going home.

Communicating as a Coach

Communication is the foundation of coaching. As a coach, nothing is more important than expressing your thoughts and ideas and relaying your knowledge and instructions effectively. You need to not only dispense information, but it has to be received and understood in order for it to matter. And as a leader and authority figure, you also need to establish strong lines of communication with various groups including parents, athletes, other coaches, school administrators, members of the community, and the media.

Communicating With Parents

Parents are an important piece of the overall puzzle. They are the greatest wellspring of support, emotionally and financially, that you are likely to have at your disposal. Because their kids are involved, parents have skin in the game. It's important to understand that. More than anything, parents want their kids to have a great experience, and they are willing to go the extra mile to make it happen. It is important to let them know who you are, what your expectations are, and how they can contact you with concerns.

Hosting a parent night before the start of the season is mandatory in many school districts, and it was certainly required at Mead. Parent night was a big deal, and it was important that it be well-organized (see figure 2.1). I scheduled it right before our time trial during the first week of practice.

I held parent night in the gym so there was always enough seating for parents in the first seven or eight rows of bleachers. I handed out a schedule for the season, including the itinerary for each meet. That way every parent knew about our bus trips, what time we were leaving school, and, of course, any hotel information. It was important to go over every detail, including discussion of our safety plan, which accounted for every athlete for the duration of every trip we took (see figure 2.2).

I also used the opportunity to explain the concept of cross country and educate parents about the sport: how it's scored, how far their kids run, and so on. You can't assume that your parents know the ins and outs of cross country, especially when their children are new to the sport.

I tried to get parents pumped up and excited for the season and seeing their kids in action doing something they love. I also chose a parent leader to be in charge of the other parents. This person organized who brought snacks on meet days—sport drinks, Popsicles, fruit—by managing a sign-up sheet and assigning parents to specific days on the

Building a Parent Army

Do what you can to encourage your parents to become as involved as possible. This is where you begin to build an army of volunteers. During the parent night, send a clipboard with a sheet around the room to get names and phone numbers and information about availability.

And then begin to ask the following:

Who can set up our team's camp at meets?

Who can put together a refreshment bar?

Who is a good photographer?

Who can take video and make a DVD?

Who can help with the awards banquet?

Who can work at the team fund-raiser?

I'll be honest. I never liked holding fund-raising events, bake sales, or car washes, but I knew that sometimes they were necessary. I was up front with my parents. I told them what we needed at the start of the season and then we passed the hat. For instance, maybe we had four kids who needed shoes. Or we needed money for hotel rooms or for a charter bus. Perhaps we were short on money for entry fees that season. Parents will usually come through and meet those needs. They will also eagerly devote their time if they have it to give.

FIGURE 2.1   Mead High School Preseason Parent Night

5:45 p.m.   Parents arrive at cafeteria to enjoy coffee, donuts, and fruit.

6:15 p.m.   Introduce staff and make opening remarks.

6:20 p.m.   Review forms to be handed in with the physical forms and remind parents to purchase an Associated Student Body Card (SB) card and pay activity fee. Review practice procedures, safety procedures, competition schedule, and standards for lettering. (Athletic director might talk about eligibility.)

6:45 p.m.   Present volunteer possibilities (sign-up sheets):

1. Helping at home cross country meets:
   - Setting up team fort (tent, tarps, water, litter bags)
   - Setting up and taking down course
   - Serving as timers, judges, spotters, and finish-line crew
   - Taking video and photos
   - Compiling team results

2. Organizing team socials and swimming parties, volunteering home for pasta feeds

3. Providing team snacks on meet days

4. Organizing and volunteering for fund-raisers, such as car washes

5. Distributing and picking up uniforms and spirit packs

6. Donating supplies for award-night potluck:
   - Freshmen and juniors—main dish
   - Sophomores—salads
   - Seniors—desert

7:15 p.m.   Show highlight video of previous season.

7:30 p.m.   Let's have a great season, "Good-bye."

---

calendar. I also invited parents to come on road trips with us or to follow our bus so that we moved down the highway like a convoy.

I welcomed parents to the Mead family and introduced each member of the coaching staff. I talked about the tradition of the program and our accomplishments, realizing that each of those parents would go back into their neighborhoods and workplaces and spread the word of what was going on with Mead cross country. I also touched on key issues. I told parents, "You have to trust us as coaches just as we trust you to be parents." Usually,

this one sentence was impactful enough. The last thing you want as a head coach is for parents to second-guess or add supplemental coaching at home after practice. If parents believe in what you're doing, that scenario is seldom a problem.

It's also important to educate parents about safety and commitment. This is the moment when you explain your expectations and distribute the team's rules. Tell your parents that you expect their support, but they should not interfere with coaching. Overzealous parents might think it's OK to pile extra workouts on

Figure 2.2 Mead High School Cross Country Safety Plan

1. The medical box will be restocked each week with the following:
   - Emergency contact cards
   - Medical adhesive tape
   - Prewrap
   - Adhesive bandages (multiple sizes)
   - Antibacterial ointment
   - Blister pads
   - Gauze pads
   - Hydrogen peroxide
   - Scissors
   - Splint
   - Two elastic bandages
   - Tape spray
   - Bee-sting kit
   - Antihistamine such as Benadryl (oral)
   - Individual first aid (e.g., inhaler, epinephrine auto-injector)
   - Gloves

2. The coach has a cell phone available at all times. It contains the assistant coaches' numbers along with the athletic director, principal, assistant principal, and athletic secretary. In the case of an emergency, 911 will be called.

3. A container of ice and ice bags will be available every day.

4. Water will be available at practice and meets, and athletes will have water bottles.

5. When running off campus, athletes will run single file on the far side of the road, usually facing oncoming traffic. Runners will make eye contact with drivers when crossing intersections when they have the right of way. Cars always win!

6. Athletes will always run in pairs or a group and never alone.

7. When running in the dark, athletes will wear reflective vests.

8. On long runs, there will be a lead runner and sweeper for safety. We want no one lost!

their child away from practice. Explain your safety concerns. Too much running can lead to injuries or fatigue, which can compound into any number of emotional and physical problems. On the other hand, lax parents might not be concerned about whether their child comes to practice regularly. Make them understand there are consequences for lack of commitment, just as there are for failing grades.

Finally, take questions to make sure parents know how to contact you when they have concerns. It's important to keep the lines of communication open and clear with parents. They should have your e-mail address and cell phone number. I made sure there was coffee at parent night plus trays of doughnuts and fresh fruit.

During the season I held regular meetings with my core group of parent volunteers who worked at our home meets. I recruited someone to work the finish chute and people to manage areas around the course. When parents are included to that extent, they become part of an infrastructure that supports the entire program.

Communicating With Athletes

Most young runners are clueless about cross country: how it works, the reasoning behind workouts, and the value of being on the team. So you have to teach them as if they were a classroom of students on their first day of French class. It takes patience. Although there is something intuitive about running, for first-timers it's a foreign language.

You must educate beginners about every aspect of the warm-up, how to prevent injuries and deal with them if necessary, how to manage their time, and how to deal with stress. You will address myriad other questions—many of which have nothing to do with cross country—that come from kids who are coming of age and figuring out their world. Some runners will ask for more of your attention. Try to find the time to give it. One option might be a weekly goal session in which you not only dole out praise, but

also are honest and suggest something that they might work on. The key to communication with athletes is to let them know they are important to the team. Be passionate about the sport and enthusiastic in your conversations.

A coach must be evenhanded and consistent when it comes to discipline. There are consequences for breaking team rules. But punishment should be followed by an opportunity to correct behavior and earn back trust.

Use the time before and after workouts to talk not only about the purpose of that day's training, but also anything else that is going on, including school dances, academics, and that week's football game. Share your thoughts. Encourage one of the team leaders to share his or her thoughts. Do what you can to maintain open lines of communication.

Before every season, I handed out printed copies of the team, practice, and competition rules that each athlete took home (figure 2.3). I would go over the content of each page and make sure that every person on the team understood the rules and knew that I expected them to be followed. These were our laws, and the laws should be both fair and firm so that everyone can abide by them.

Figure 2.3 Team, Practice, and Competition Rules

TEAM RULES

- You are expected to abide by the Mead High School athletic code.
- If you require physiotherapy, medical attention, or general training, you must follow the certified trainer's program to the letter.
- You should strive to establish your individual suitable weight (and percentage of body fat). The coaching staff and other professionals will help you determine what that is.
- You are expected to have an organized and up-to-date training diary.
- You are expected to set performance goals and plan your steps to success. To succeed in competition and in Mead Panther cross country, you must take care of both your body and mind. You must attempt to do your best every day: That's all it takes, in athletics and life. Enjoy the satisfaction of honest effort and being part of our team. If you have reservations about your commitment, please talk to a coach.

> *continued*

Team, Practice, and Competition Rules   > continued

PRACTICE RULES

- Team practices begin at 2:50 sharp in the location designated. If you cannot attend a practice, you must see the coach beforehand. You may not send someone with a message for the coach.
- You will participate in all the training unless you have been provided a special program by the coach.
- If you are ill or injured, see the coach at the beginning of training. Otherwise 100 percent effort is expected.
- Mentally prepare for each practice by reviewing your practice goals so you can gain from each experience.
- Always come to practice in acceptable gear.
- When your teammates are participating in fatiguing training, your encouragement is valuable and expected. You'll in turn appreciate their support during your most challenging moments.
- Vince Lombardi said, "Fatigue makes cowards of us all." And he's right, so be as brave as you can for as long as you can, and you'll be amazed at how long, how far, and how fast you can go.

COMPETITION RULES

- We wear only Mead gear throughout our competitive experience. We run for the Mead Panthers. We wear Mead Panther apparel. Other apparel is unacceptable.
- Tuck in your jersey.
- Compete and behave with pride and class from the first moment we arrive until we depart, regardless of outcomes.

Pat Tyson (right) shares a thought with assistant coach and former Mead runner Yukon Degenhart (left).

Communicating With Assistant Coaches

It's important that you and your assistant coaches maintain a unified front because division in the ranks is never good for morale. Talk to your assistants often, listen to their input and their concerns, and let them know that their time and effort are valued. I enjoyed sitting down with coaches on road trips, sometimes in a hotel room or in the lobby or over a meal to discuss what was going well and what needed more attention. I gave my assistants lots of wiggle room to do the things that they were good at for the benefit of the team. Nobody likes a micromanager.

I often set goals for my assistants and asked them to set their own goals and share them with me. Sometimes it is difficult to share a weakness or an area that needs significant improvement, but you need to be honest with your assistants. If you think they are being too hard on a kid or not firm enough, talk about it in a weekly discussion or a postmeet discussion. Your assistants have to be people you can be direct and honest with. Otherwise, it won't work.

Communicating With Other Teachers and Administrators

Cultivating friendships with the physical education teachers at your school can be an extremely valuable tool for recruiting kids to come out for the team. The physical education teachers, in many cases, are the first adults at a school to evaluate the physical abilities of students, particularly the freshmen.

My college track coach Bill Bowerman went to the area high schools and asked the physical education teachers to give five tests to all their students: 800 meters, 400 meters, softball throw, jump-reach, and standing broad jump. The last three tests indicated success in field events for the spring track season, but the 800 and the 400 helped evaluate prospective middle- and long-distance runners. Then he took the data, and from those tests, he categorized each athlete. I have gotten physical education teachers to do that, too, usually after bribing them with a gift card or coupon for something they want.

School counselors are also a great asset. New kids move in or exchange students arrive, and counselors are eager to get them involved with the school. Cross country is a great place to make that happen. And if a counselor knows you or has other kids who enjoy cross country, then they will steer new students to you. I made a point of going to the counselors and asking for the names of new students. I didn't care whether they were runners or not. It never hurts to ask a new kid to try out a practice or two. If kids give it a try and like it, you could possibly keep them for four years. If they don't enjoy it, that's OK, too. At least they'll know and so will you.

Other teachers can identify students who might make good candidates for cross country, as well. Go to a faculty meeting and give teachers a short blurb you'd like them to read in class or put up on their classroom wall about joining the cross country team. More often than not, the teachers will be willing to help you. Don't forget to take snacks to the faculty meeting. You need the teachers to like you.

I considered myself lucky to have had administrators that loved all sports and treated cross country the same as football. The superintendent of schools came by in the morning for our run, and he was not a jogger. He even came to our state meet. I know that doesn't happen everywhere. But you have to give it a shot and try to connect with them. Some of them may not join in, but others will.

After a while, you may get to a point where the student body president is a runner, and the editor of the yearbook is a runner, and it snowballs. Identity as a member of the cross country team begins to carry weight and credibility throughout the building.

Communicating With Others in Your Community

I enjoyed meeting the coaches of the youth programs in the area and building relationships with them. Be aware of what's going on in the feeder schools. The youth coaches can be valuable assets and also help amplify the message of what your program stands for. Invite them to drop by practice and show them what your team is about, tell them your goals, and let them be a part of it. Ask them to come to a clinic or coaching workshop. Tell them the important dates on the calendar, and encourage them to bring their young kids to meets so they can watch and be inspired.

I took a group of middle school kids to the state meet during track season to work on the hurdle crew. These sixth-, seventh-, and eighth-graders experienced the state meet up close and saw what excellence looked like. I also welcomed them to our annual postseason award banquet. By reaching out to the younger kids in the area and showing them what cross country is like, you plant that seed early. That way, when those kids arrive for their first day of high school, they already know what cross country is and whether they want to be part of it. That is crucial, because in most cases across the United Sates, high school freshmen don't have any idea what the sport of cross country is.

Communicating With the Press

I have met a lot of high school cross country coaches who bemoan the fact that their local newspapers don't report their news or their results. I have met other coaches who are persistent squeaky wheels and have managed to get items into the paper by the sheer force of their tenacity.

Big-city daily newspapers and TV stations do not rush out to cover cross country. Small newspapers that cover high school sports extensively might be eager for your information, but they might be staffed by people who don't care much about cross country.

It never hurts to send e-mails to local reporters who might be interested in a schedule before the season starts, a link to results after a meet, or a few sentences about a news angle. There's no reason to act desperate for coverage or oversell a story idea. A story idea will either interest someone or it won't. If a reporter has interest in learning more, invite him or her to practice. As a coach, it is your responsibility to be the spokesperson for your program. Take that job seriously. Cultivate the members of the press who express interest and always be friendly and positive while dispensing your information.

Occasionally, my athletes got on the local TV station for activities outside of cross country season, like fund-raisers for the homeless or involvement in a litter pickup campaign. The press may be more interested in those stories than they are about your result at the state championship. Just remember, if you don't build relationships with the people likely to amplify your team's story, they'll never find out on their own.

Developing a Travel Plan

In all of my time as a coach I always felt it was important for athletes to travel to the competition together on the bus and travel back to school on the bus when the meet was over.

This is a safety issue, making sure that each student is accounted for coming and going. And also, the bus is an extension of the clubhouse. When we prepared for a meet and celebrated its outcome or endured the agony of defeat, we did it together. This sort of policy isn't enforced everywhere and sometimes it isn't feasible. At some schools, the bus is available to get to the meet but not available afterward. In that case, there is little choice but to let the students find their own way home with parents, grandparents, or friends. I still recommend gathering the team at the end of the meet, breaking down what happened, bringing closure to it, and making sure that everyone has a ride. At Mead, 99 percent of the time we all went to the meet together, and 99 percent of the time we came home together.

Travel rules (figure 2.4) are important because your team is outside of its usual safe zone. There are variables that come into play on the road. Unfamiliar people and unfamiliar surroundings can become unexpected hazards. You can never be too careful when you are charged with the safety of teenagers, some of whom are intent on pushing boundaries.

Figure 2.4 Travel Rules

- When traveling by van, bus, or plane, dress in a manner that represents Mead cross country and Mead High School appropriately.

- You will travel to and from a competition site with the team. In extraordinary situations, the coach may release you directly to your parents and no one else.

- If you must go anywhere unscheduled (e.g., leave the competition site, gas station, motel) you must let the coach know why and how long you will be. We don't want to lose you.

- You may wear billed hats (baseball caps), but only if they are related to Mead or Mead cross country. Once we arrive at the competition site, put your cap in your bag until we are back on the bus to return to school.

- Take responsibility for equipment that needs to be carried on trips (e.g., tarps, medical kit, tent). Don't wait for coaches to carry equipment or ask you to do it. Help our team by doing work that you see needs to be done.

- It is important to keep the Mead High School vans and buses clean. Always pick up garbage and leave the vehicle clean.

- The coach may assign roommates.

- We represent ourselves, Mead High School, the Greater Spokane League, the State of Washington, and at times the United States. Always conduct yourself with this in mind. We want to be friendly, disciplined, poised, and well-groomed. We want people to say, "These are people we respect and whom we'd like to know."

Competing Against Other Sports for Athletes

One of the first junior high runners I had when I started coaching was a girl named Michelle Akers. She was the coolest girl and a very good runner, too. But cross country wasn't her long-term goal. She became one of the greatest female soccer players of all time, scoring 105 goals for the U.S. women's team. She starred during the 1991 and 1999 World Cup tournaments and was probably the top American woman in the sport until Mia Hamm came along.

At Mead, I would have loved having a guy like Adam Morrison come out for the team. He was one of the most competitive kids I've seen, a real killer. But his sport was basketball, and at Gonzaga, he led the NCAA in scoring during the 2005-06 season.

High school students have a variety of sports to choose from, and their time is limited. So kids should be allowed to participate in whatever sport gives them joy. As a cross country coach, all you can do is show them what the sport is about and how it feels to be a member of the team and let them decide whether they have a passion for it.

Sometimes soccer players come out for cross country practice and fall in love with it or discover they have more talent for it. Some don't. High school boys' soccer in Washington is a spring activity. In many other states,

cross country and soccer programs go head to head on the fall calendar and competition exists among coaches for the top available athletes as soccer players can also make great runners. Our sport has lost a good many runners to soccer. Occasionally, athletes discover a talent for running on the soccer pitch and find their way into cross country.

Another source of competition for an athlete's time is club-sport programs that demand students to devote time and resources to nonschool teams. I'm a proponent of school sports and representing your high school. I'm not knocking community sports, but I have a hard time accepting hockey or soccer coaches controlling kids year-round, or in some cases most of the year, and discouraging them from representing their schools in other sports. Sometimes those sorts of politics come into play. My advice is to build a program and create a culture that speaks for itself and attracts the athletes who want to be there.

Some principals don't want coaches to "own" the athletes and enforce that aim through policies. If I had told a kid at Mead that he couldn't play soccer, I know I would have gotten into trouble. And the band instructor would have gotten in trouble for telling musicians that they couldn't join cross country. I think it's always better for coaches and other school leaders to be supportive of one another. It's better for school spirit, and it puts less stress on the students.

Summary

Developing communication skills and building relationships is essential to finding success as a coach in any sport. In cross country, try to engage several important constituencies.

- Build rapport with athletes by showing a genuine interest in their goals and dreams and then show them how you can help them get where they want to be.

- Create a clubhouse of some kind that is a team sanctuary, a place that embodies the spirit of the group and is inclusive and welcoming to everybody in the program.

- Make sure that other adults in your school—teachers, counselors, and other coaches—understand what you and your team represent and what sort of students you are looking for.

- Recognize that parents are a great resource for emotional support and for fund-raising and as a volunteer pool. Parents will go to great lengths to make sure their children are happy and healthy, and if they believe in the direction of your program and clearly understand the goals and the process, they can become a tremendous asset. Engage parents with confidence and enthusiasm, but also draw a distinct line between your responsibilities as coach and theirs as parents.

CHAPTER 3 Motivating Runners

I never saw much of my father and have very few memories of him. He and my mother split up when I was little, and I can remember the day when relatives stopped by the house to tell my mom that he had died. I was outside, hiding under the porch when they gave her the news. I was seven.

I lived in a low-income neighborhood in Tacoma, Washington. I wore the same clothes every day because I didn't know any better. I inserted small scraps of cardboard into my shoes to cover the holes in the bottoms of them. My mom never had a car. We took the bus everywhere, which was never very far. I was the youngest of four kids, and after my father died of cancer, I was the kid who was the pleaser. I wanted to do everything that I could to make my mom happy.

I was an average student through grade school and junior high, and I never missed a day of school. Although my mother was loving, there was no academic environment at home, and I was insecure about my place in the world. Only 3 or 4 percent of my classmates went on to college. Everyone else looked forward to graduating and going straight into the military, which at that time meant a tour of duty in Vietnam, or getting married and going to work in the shipyard or in a mill or in the tidal flats.

In my teen years, I found a father figure in Dan Watson, the track coach at Lincoln High School. He was a former Colorado state champ in the 100-yard dash and earned his degree from Northern Colorado. He came west to get his master's degree at Oregon State and took an interest in the University of Oregon track and field team, and he made frequent trips to watch meets at Hayward Field.

Coach Watson was my greatest influence in choosing to become a coach. He was dedicated to building a strong program that was organized to last year-round. Instead of promoting a three-month commitment in the fall or spring, Coach Watson showed me that running was a lifestyle. He required us to keep a training journal and he left copies of *Track and Field News* around his office where we could pick them up and read them. He also took us to track meets in Seattle. I can remember watching Gerry Lindgren nearly breaking the world record for the 3 mile (4.8 km) on a dirt track in the rain and wind on a cold day in 1966.

Lindgren, New Zealand's Bill Bailey, Australia's Ron Clarke, and Washington's Doris Brown Heritage—runners I saw at Seattle's big indoor meet—became my heroes. They were, for me, what Mickey Mantle and Whitey Ford were to other kids. Coach Watson exposed me to excellence. The entire time I was thinking, "Oh, man, that was so cool! I want to be like that!"

One of my older Lincoln teammates went to community college in Spokane, and he invited me over to that part of the state for the weekend. I got on a train at 8:00 p.m. and got there at 8:00 a.m. I trained with Ferris kids or Rogers kids, and I met two of my heroes, Rick Riley and Gerry Lindgren. I loved hanging around with winners, and I made connections with them.

When I was a sophomore, I finished between 150th and 160th at the state cross country meet. I was still new to the sport, straining to grasp how it all worked. I'd go out like Forrest Gump, just run hard and pray I'd hold on. I always ran like that. My development accelerated when Coach Watson asked me to train with an older runner from Mount Tahoma High School named Sam Ring.

I was intimidated by Sam. To me, he was a rock star. Every time I'd go on 10-mile (16 km) runs with him, he'd beat me up with his legs and his words. He'd call me names when I struggled to stay up with him. I'd come home from those runs sick to my stomach, sometimes humiliated. But Sam didn't give up on me, and I was determined to prove my worthiness. Over time, I improved and I got tougher. As a junior I was 18th at the state cross country meet, and as a senior I was 7th. In the spring, I broke the school records in the mile (4:24) and the two mile (9:22).

Getting Started in College

During my senior year at Lincoln, I applied to the University of Oregon, Oregon State, the University of Washington, Washington State, Central Washington, and Highline Community College. I was accepted to all of them and offered generous financial-aid packages. I essentially had a full ride to Washington State, and because my idols Lindgren and Riley had gone there, I decided in the spring of my senior year that I wanted to go there, too. However, a chance encounter with an Oregon assistant coach later in the year caused me to change my mind.

After the state track championships, I got a ride down to a postseason all-star meet in Lake Oswego, Oregon, that brought together athletes from Oregon, Washington, and Idaho. Bill Dellinger, the assistant coach at Oregon, was there and somehow I had the guts to go up and introduce myself to him. During that conversation I asked, "Is there a chance I could run for Oregon?" And he said, "Yes."

It was Coach Watson's dream for one of his athletes to go to the University of Oregon, and so I took a risk and investigated my chances of making it there. Bill Dellinger invited me to come down to Eugene to watch the Low-Altitude Training Meet on August 1 at Hayward Field. The event was held as a preview of the athletes who would soon vie to make the 1968 U.S. Olympic team in Echo Summit, California, near Lake Tahoe to simulate Mexico City's 8,000-foot (2,400 m) elevation.

It became a three-day weekend that I'll never forget. The recruit invited to share the dorm room with me was a high school junior from Coos Bay, Oregon, named Steve Prefontaine. We watched the meet together from the stands at Hayward Field. The highlight was a 5,000-meter showdown between Lindgren and Oregon's own distance standout, Kenny Moore. When Moore won, the place erupted. I'd never seen anything like it. I got chills up and down my spine and so did the kid next to me. He couldn't stop talking about it.

When I went to Springfield to meet Dellinger and his wife, Marol, I ate at their dinner table. Then he pulled out a film reel of one of his greatest races (he was the bronze medalist at the 1964 Olympics in the 5,000 meters) and played it for me. I was mesmerized just to be in his presence. That was my official visit. I was sold on the University of Oregon.

Motivating Myself at Oregon

The head coach at Oregon was an imposing figure named Bill Bowerman, and he probably didn't say two words to me during my first six months on campus. I was "hamburger," which is what he called all of the wannabes and hangers-on that wanted to prove they were worthy to one day wear the Oregon jersey at Hayward Field.

One of my very first encounters with Bowerman was rather unpleasant. He came to me during the spring of my freshman year and said I'd be a better fit for Oregon as a manager than I would as a runner. I was crushed, but later I got his full attention in a positive way by continually beating my personal best times and making the varsity cross country team. I kept trying because I had the desire to achieve. I was chasing my dream, and one comment wouldn't keep me from it. Much the same way Sam Ring had goaded me into digging deeper and not giving up, Bowerman had pushed a button in me. I would have done almost anything to win his acceptance and approval. I wasn't a quitter. My persistence kept me focused on chasing my dream.

Taking the Pied Piper Approach

The model of what a college program should look and feel like was all around me when I was at the University of Oregon. Motivation was simple. You either produced results or you got left behind. Bowerman presided over the team as an authoritarian godlike figure, there to encourage but also end your dream and suggest you become the manager if he thought it might increase your focus and dedication.

When I became a coach, first in a junior high and later high school, I had no intention of emulating Bill Bowerman. First of all, that's not my personality. Second, with younger athletes, I don't think it would be terribly successful. Bowerman applied pressure to his athletes and pushed them beyond their imagined limits, and his methods produced legendary success. But as a recipient of that pressure, I didn't enjoy the stress. I decided to approach coaching in a vastly different way.

While I was at Mead, a Spokane newspaper writer referred to me as a Pied Piper, meaning that I had a knack for speaking to kids in a way that they understood, holding their attention, and leading them in the direction I wanted

them to go. When I think of the Pied Piper approach to coaching, I'm referring to a style of coaching that attracts kids who want to be connected to something fun, positive, and life changing. It's evangelizing for the sport of running, and pulling in kids who believe in the program.

Not everyone has the personality to pull this off. Some of the very best cross country coaches have quiet personalities. They may have all of the knowledge and strategies to build successful programs, but they don't have the charisma of a Pied Piper. A coach who doesn't have that personality has to find a Pied Piper who is willing to join and be an assistant coach, someone who is able and willing to be out there, loud and boisterous, as a recruiter. It's important to find that person if you want to build your program. You need a magnet.

I don't think I always was a Piper, but I figured out that if I brought lots of energy to the table, I could make a difference in the lives of the young people around me. Kids love being around positively charged people. I drew on my personal motivations, from people like Bill Bowerman, Bill Dellinger, and Steve Prefontaine, and I went to clinics and heard motivational speakers. To this day, I still do that.

If you don't summon high energy naturally, go hear someone speak who inspires you, perhaps at a local college campus or a summer running camp, or read about someone fascinating. If there is something that you can do to get energized, you can begin to feed it to your athletes. One thing you can't do is fake it. Kids know when someone is phony. You can work on being more charismatic around others, but it will ring hollow if your enthusiasm isn't genuine.

Positively Motivating

Motivation should happen every day in cross country. Every member of the team should be motivated to achieve his or her personal goals. The team should be motivated to win the next invitational, to move up in the rankings, to ultimately win the state championship.

But motivation doesn't come out of thin air. Some kids want to compete more than others. Some are driven either by an internal motor or external pressures to stay hungry for success. I tried to use unrelenting positivity as a motivating force. I preached that being a runner who has adopted the running lifestyle was something worth striving for. I tried to make it a cool activity. Everybody was on time today for practice? That's a win! Two-thirds of the freshmen just ran personal bests? Another win! The varsity guys just completed a workout they did two weeks ago, only this time a couple seconds faster per interval? Guys, we're winning!

Kids feed off enthusiasm, and so once they get into a pattern of doing things right and seeing improvement in their results, they like the feel of it. Usually, they pick up the motivation to continue to seek progress on their own in an environment like that.

Leading the Charge

As the coach, you are the maestro of motivation. You have a chance to make each kid on the team feel special about his or her effort and feel valued as a member of the team and stay focused on the next goal.

How do you give every kid your attention? Here's how:

1. Strike up a banter with the kids. Tease them a little bit, find the common ground, bring them into your tribe or your energy, and you'll be amazed how quickly they will buy in. When you give kids your undivided attention, they will respond in a positive way.

2. Pipers have a high-powered ability to energize. Be fired up about the moment, fired up about the kids, fired up about the school. That gets a kid fired up, and that kid goes, "Wow, I want to be part of that!"

3. Take kids to watch something that sparks their imagination. Show them an inspirational movie or videos of great races. Take them to see a college meet or a championship of some kind.

Exposing kids to something special, something eye opening, can have a profound impact on their growing interest and commitment.

4. At Mead, kids needed the Monday-night pizza gatherings. At other schools, there is something else. A bowling night. A movie night. Whatever it is, find a way to bring your athletes together for something fun and social. It is a good thing for the rookies and helps plant the seed. You have to show them something awesome that they want to be part of. As a coach, you create these moments based on the culture that is in place in your program.

5. Find the success in everything that you do. Talk about how each small accomplishment is another log on the fire. This is how you begin to create momentum from one day to the next all season long. By the time late October comes around, your team is riding a cresting wave of emotion, motivation, and desire that leads to success.

Making an Extra Effort

How do you reach kids who seem distant or unmotivated? It can be a challenge, and sometimes being a high-energy person draws them near but not all the way in. You have to work at gaining their trust. You can do that by taking the time to learn more about them and where they come from. That is one of the best ways to build a positive relationship.

If a hard case was someone I felt needed to be involved and on the team, I might have gone on a run with him at an easy pace, one on one. That was an investment in time and energy. Also, handwritten notes thanking runners for their commitment or commending their effort was effective. Over the course of a year, I wrote hundreds of notes, and I found them to be a valuable tool for touching base with someone. It was effective because it was personal and it was something they could file away and hold onto.

Motivation That Works

My old coach Bill Dellinger used to ask me, "What is the most important ingredient of a very good runner?" My answer was "A huge amount of desire!" Yes, talent is a significant part of the mix. Yet there are many examples of talented runners who lacked desire or were distracted and did not reach their potential.

Some high school runners across the country push themselves by sheer willpower. Some of them come from schools so small they don't have cross country teams to run on. Others don't have tracks to run on. Still they persist, finding ways to do workouts by themselves if necessary. They set goals and go after them. A motivated runner finds a way.

In cross country, a runner doesn't rely solely on his or her own motivation. A team of runners can share the emotional, spiritual, and inspirational load. Teammates run not only for themselves but also for each other.

If you can create a culture at your school in which running is cool, that is a powerful motivator as well. But let's be perfectly honest. The cross country kids in a typical high school are quite often not regarded by their peers with the same respect or awe as the football

Matt Davis had a rare combination of talent and desire, and his example motivated the runners who followed him in the Mead tradition.

and basketball players. That's why it takes work to build something that has the cachet of cool and respect throughout the school.

I wore T-shirts from the Olympic Trials. It showed my kids right away that I was connected to something bigger and deeper in the sport. Find ways to teach kids about the history of running. Tell them about Roger Bannister and the elusive sub-4:00 mile. Show them video of Billy Mills winning the gold medal in the 10,000 meters in 1964. Show them recent video of Galen Rupp and Mo Farah displaying teamwork in the 2012 London Games. Help them understand who Haile Gebrselassie and Hicham El Guerrouj are. Encourage them to tune in to watch the New York or Boston Marathons and tell them the backstories of women like Shalane Flanagan and Kara Goucher. Once a high school runner begins to understand the concept of pace and how fast they run and can compare that to the fastest runners in the country and around the world, they begin to grasp the fuller context of the sport.

Sometimes you can fire up your team's internal motivation by showing them what they are part of and what different levels of success look like. I used to feed my top-seven runners kernels of information about what it would take for them to qualify for Nike Cross Nationals, which helped plant the seed and began to motivate them.

Not everything works. Some kids just simply don't have the same desire that you have. All you can do as a coach is give it your best shot. You don't have to overdo it. You will find that some kids need a little bit more space and time. They will come aboard if you play it more low key in the beginning. Different kids respond to coaching in different ways. Some love a high-energy pep talk. Others need something more subtle. Do what you can to learn your athletes' styles.

Learning From Steve Prefontaine

The story of Steve Prefontaine remains a huge source of motivation for young runners who have seen the movies *Prefontaine* or *Without Limits*. Some kids have his poster in their bedrooms or read inspirational quotes by him. I remember him as an inspirational guy. He made you want to follow his lead. You can use Pre's life story as motivation for your athletes, or perhaps there is a personal or public hero in your own life that you can use.

In addition to fuel for inspiration, there are several practical lessons that I learned from my time with Pre. What follows are tips on running and life that I attribute to him.

1. **Establish rhythm.** Training and daily life have a rhythm. One of Pre's most distinguishing characteristics was his ability to manage his time. His life was organized. It had consistent rhythm. He woke up at 6:00 a.m. and was out the door at 6:10 for the morning run. He got in the car, drove to campus, attended classes, and then went to practice at 2:30. Then he went back to the trailer or to dinner and then to bed. It wasn't random, and it was always consistent. He was always in bed by 10:00 p.m. There was time, occasionally, to go out and relax, to do something spontaneous like go to Dairy Queen for two-for-one banana splits, but the rhythm always took over again.

2. **Maintain perspective.** Pre said to me, "You worry too much." He used to call me a worrywart. He'd say to me, "Why don't you just lighten up? It will make you a better runner." I have taken those words to heart. As a coach or a runner, we're not flying $50 million jets and landing them on an aircraft carrier. What we're doing is all simple stuff. Pre knew when to turn it on and turn it off, when to be stupid and silly, and when to get ready. He kept himself busy on meet days, but usually around 1:00 p.m. on Saturdays, he would put his game face on to be ready for his race at 3 p.m. He'd go for a light jog in the morning, clean the trailer, and clean his car, always staying busy. When he kept himself busy he didn't think about the race. Then, on the way to the race, he got in the zone.

3. **Know your body.** Pre had the ability to relax and keep from taking his races too seriously. He tried to avoid becoming robotic. He didn't want to think too much about racing and all the scenarios that could go wrong. Instead, he'd line up and be ready for anything, relying on his instincts to kick in as the race unfolded.

When I ran with Pre he always asked me, "How do you feel?" And so I always responded, "Oh, I feel great!" I said that even if I didn't feel great. And during those runs, always under 6:00-per-mile pace, I was always a little tired, but I kept going because that's just what I did. He thought anything over 6:00 per mile wouldn't do any good. He ran with focus and intensity.

4. **Listen to your body.** When Pre asked, "How do you feel?" his intention was to make sure I was listening to my body. He was a master at it. He had instant radar that told him something was starting to go wrong. I've never met anyone who had that sort of sensitivity. I think it's why in the story of Steve Prefontaine's running career, there is practically no mention of injuries. In four years at Oregon, he never missed a race and never missed a workout.

It's easy to say to a kid, "Err on the side of doing less" to avoid an injury. But what does that mean to a 15-, 16-, 17-year-old kid? It's a fine line, and you have to make sure you don't overdo it. There needs to be a day or two every week to go easy. Pre understood that there was something called conversation pace. If you couldn't talk, you were going too fast.

5. **Trust the system.** I never had to wonder how Pre would answer a question or solve a problem about training. I knew instinctively what he would do, how he would respond. I feel like that came from Bill Dellinger, our coach at Oregon. Pre never questioned workouts from Dellinger. He showed up for practice with his lunch pail and did exactly what he was supposed to do that day. I think

that we all answer challenges and problems the same way. We don't shy away from them. We do what has to be done and trust the outcome.

6. **Learn how to focus.** Some athletes on race day never see their glass as half full. It's always half empty. Pre was different. He never allowed negativity to enter his thoughts before a race. On race day, he visualized, either sitting or lying down, and when the time came, he hopped in the car and was on his way to the meet. He completely focused at that point. You could see it in his eyes and the way he carried his body. He was getting ready to go on stage. However, he didn't start to get psyched up about the race until two and a half or three hours before it. Some athletes turn on a day or two ahead of time. That's too early.

I use music to get my kids pumped up on the way to a meet. Some athletes have a particular song that puts them into a frenzy. I drove our runners to the state meet. We never got there too early, and I kept them away from the course until we needed to be there. Sometimes being there too early can wear on runners.

7. **Nerves are fine.** Pre wasn't negative about the potential outcome of a race, but he did sometimes say, "I don't feel good today." I think it was nerves more than anything else, because everyone gets them before a big race. His way of showing his nerves was to say, "I don't feel good today," and then go out and blow everybody away. I can't recall one time when he said he didn't feel good before a race that he didn't turn around and have a great performance.

When kids come up to me before a race and say they don't feel good, their stomachs are queasy, I tell them that's awesome. It means you're going to have a great race.

8. **See it in the eyes.** There was an unmistakable look in Pre's eyes that I paid close attention to, and it's always fas-cinated me. I saw it occasionally in the high school kids that I coached at Mead and also in runners on other teams. It's confidence. It's fearlessness. It is edginess and a willingness to go out on the course and run aggressively. It's a very interesting thing, and every coach at some point will have an athlete who has it.

9. **Let go of the reins.** One of the things I admired about Bill Dellinger was that he let Pre become Pre. He let him do what he needed to do. There were no rules. Dellinger took the stance "Let's see what Pre can do without rules." It was freedom. I took that philosophy from Coach Dellinger. Let the kids be radical and make mistakes.

When I coached Matt Davis as a sophomore he always hit a 60-second third lap in the 1,600 meters and then faltered badly on the fourth. Eventually he mastered that pace and was able to sustain it, and that fourth lap became easier by his senior year. I liked that. When you try to control your runners, that's when kids start to lose their instincts.

10. **Discipline matters.** Pre was especially disciplined. He never took days off, never missed runs on Sundays. In fact, some Sundays he added a second short run later in the day. That extra run was so that he knew he was getting an edge on his opponents. I know that some very well-educated running coaches will say going seven days a week is too much and that rest days need to be built in. Pre didn't take days off. Some days were just lighter than others.

11. **Feed off of the competition.** The best runners need to know where the bar is set. Pre had Jim Ryun and Gerry Lindgren to look up to. They set the standard that Pre tried to emulate and then exceed. He fed off those comparisons. Pre became the measuring stick for guys in the 1970s like Craig Virgin, Alberto Salazar, and Rudy Chapa. The same thing has happened in the past

dozen years. Alan Webb and Dathan Ritzenhein came along and set the standard for Chris Solinsky, Galen Rupp, German Fernandez, and Lukas Verzbicas to chase after. Similarly, pioneering women like Doris Brown Heritage, Debbie Heald, and Joan Benoit Samuelson created legacies for Lynn Jennings and Mary Slaney, and in turn for Jordan Hasay and Mary Cain.

In Pre's day, the best way to keep track of what someone else was doing was through copies of *Track and Field News* magazine. Today the communication is practically instantaneous. The Internet has created virtual communities and race results, videos, and interviews are readily available.

Some of the items in this list are not so intuitive today, so I include them for your consideration. This was how Pre saw the world, and it's how he operated. I frequently think back on these lessons and take peace of mind from them. I'm convinced there was genius in his running, and I've been calling upon that wisdom ever since he died.

What Would Steve Prefontaine Do?

Steve Prefontaine, my former college teammate and roommate, has been dead for nearly 40 years. And yet, as I travel from coast to coast for high school running clinics each summer, I see signs that he has never been more alive. He remains an inspirational force, an ideal for grit, determination, cool, and excellence all rolled into one. Pre had a swagger and charisma that could move stadiums. He got a look in his eye that told you he was unbeatable, a locomotive engine that used the force of willpower to win races just as much as he used his legs and lungs.

In April of 1969, as a senior at Marshfield High School, Prefontaine broke Rick Riley's U.S. high school two-mile record by almost seven seconds when he ran 8:41.5 at the Corvallis Invitational. His huge talent gained even more fame over the coming months

when he made the U.S. national team and earned the right to compete in Europe fresh out of high school. By the time he entered the University of Oregon in the fall of 1969, he was one of the most famous runners in the country.

His first couple of years on campus, I didn't know him very well. He associated primarily with the guys who could push him in workouts. As time went on that was an ever-diminishing number of upperclassmen. It wasn't until the fall of 1971 that I settled in and gained some traction in the program. I became the third man on the Oregon cross country team, and the fact that I was running well is probably what put me on Pre's radar. After we won the NCAA Championship that fall, Pre decided to take the next nine months off from the University of Oregon and concentrate on making the 1972 Olympic team.

One day the telephone rang in my apartment and I picked it up. It was Pre. He wanted to know whether I would be interested in sharing a single-wide trailer with him about three miles (4.8 km) east of campus. I thought about it for a moment. I had just moved in with another guy on the team, and this would affect him as well. But I also knew that Pre must have put some careful thought into whom he wanted to ask. If he felt I was the right guy, then I felt I owed it to him to try it out.

That began our friendship and our 18 months as roommates. But during the time that we shared those accommodations, I had a peek behind the curtain and into the genuine and private life of one of America's greatest athletes. Our friendship evolved into something more like family. We became close as brothers. I went to Coos Bay with him and saw the blue-collar background that had shaped him. I saw his dedication to being great counterbalanced by his fear of losing and letting "his people" down.

There isn't a day that goes by that I don't think about Steve Prefontaine and the lessons I learned from observing him. In 1972, while I lived with him, he finished fourth in the 5,000 meters at the Munich Olympic Games at just 21 years old.

Friends Steve Prefontaine (left) and Pat Tyson (right) warm up together prior to a meet in the early 1970s.

In the blink of an eye, it seemed, he was gone. One night he was racing at Hayward Field in front of his crowd, delivering another virtuoso performance. By the next morning, after the convertible car he was driving hit an embankment and flipped over on top of him, he was dead. He was only 24 years old. I grieved that loss far more than I had the death of my father when I was seven.

No matter how much time goes by, I still feel a profoundly deep connection to Pre. His life is an endless source of motivation to me and a reminder that each day is precious. One of his famous quotations was "To give anything less than your best is to sacrifice the gift." I try to live those words and apply them to my coaching. Each day is a gift. Each kid in your program is a gift. Don't waste them!

me for the past 40 years. I know many coaches who never knew Pre, and many athletes who were born long after he died, who have found inspiration in him that have kept his memory alive. But I also know that there are many other ways to motivate young runners. Acts of heroism happen every day. Athletes go to great lengths to show their compassion and sportsmanship.

Any time there is an opportunity to run with an inspired heart, the burden of the work feels lifted. Even more beautiful is the day that comes when your athletes are motivated and inspired by one another.

I also used external motivation by dangling carrots, or rewards, for achievement. I awarded special T-shirts to the runners who earned them through commitment and by beating personal records. They were black and said Mead Cross Country on the front in bold white letters. A line from Shakespeare was printed on the back. I gave those shirts to kids who never missed a day during winter training. I offered it again to kids who were committed to running all summer without missing a workout. I also offered shirts designed with images of Pre or Mead legends. Those were for the guys I called our Dirty Dozen, the select few who reached the top of the program. The kids wanted them, and they worked hard for them. Also, I invited those same committed kids to summer camps or off-season adventures. A select few runners earned these perks through hard work and they were an indicator of advancement or success.

Ultimately, motivation isn't caused by the ability to earn a T-shirt. It's something that comes from within, and the shirt is simply validation. More than anything, I wanted to motivate my athletes to strive for three things that didn't have much to do with running: Be kind. Live a meaningful life. Work on your weaknesses.

Putting It All Together

Steve Prefontaine is important to me, and my memories are a wellspring of inspiration that I have tried to share with the people around

Summary

Motivation is fuel, like gasoline or food, for a runner's soul. Whether it comes naturally or as the byproduct of inspiration or a pep talk or a fear of failure, it's the coach's job to manage motivation and know how it affects athletes.

- Examine your own story and background and explore who influenced and motivated you as an athlete. Recognize the people that you strive to emulate or differ from as a coach.

- To become a Pied Piper, use high energy and positivity to attract kids who want to be around you and be part of your club.

- Even if you don't have a big, charismatic personality, gain kids' trust by giving them your undivided attention and showing them that you care.

- Steve Prefontaine remains a source of inspiration to runners everywhere for a variety of reasons. Borrow from his life story or find another example to fire the imaginations of your runners.

- External motivation in the form of special T-shirts or other perks can become tangible goals for runners seeking the next level.

- Inspiration exists not only to fuel a runner's courage, but also to affect the choices and behaviors outside of athletics, hopefully for the betterment of the person.

CHAPTER 4

Building a Cross Country Program

In cross country, the number of athletes who come out for the team is paramount. The more athletes you have to work with, the more likely you are to find seven with the talent and drive to be successful. Cross country should be as inclusive as possible. For some students, cross country is a way to manage weight. For others, it provides an opportunity to be social and connected to something larger. But cross country is also competitive, and the more competitors you have trying to make varsity, the harder it will be for them to actually make it. Making the varsity top seven becomes something that your slower athletes aspire to.

Recruiting

Recruiting is where the Piped Piper approach and appeal, discussed in chapter 3, pays dividends. The strength of your personality, the warmth and excitement you exude, all matter.

Mobilize your assistant coaches, your school's physical education teachers, school counselors, and teaching friends to help you. When these key people understand the value and experience that comes from cross country, they will keep an eye out and recommend your program to the kids who seem like the right fit.

Having a job at the school where you coach is a tremendous advantage. You are free to patrol the hallways and locate young students who don't yet participate in extracurricular activities. Banter with them. Sell cross country by explaining the most appealing aspects of the program: the trips, the winning, and the school spirit. Your goal is to find kids who are motivated to try it. You don't need to sentence them to prison if it turns out they don't like it. The kids who come out for two or three days and decide that cross country isn't for them are more than likely not the committed characters that you want.

Physical education teachers often hold assessments during the first week or two of class, and that often includes a running test. If these teachers are friends of yours and understand what you are offering in cross country, they will approach their top-performing kids and send them straight to you.

Cross country is a numbers game, and the more runners who are willing to work at it in order to be part of the team, the better.

Outfitting a Team

There is something about the gear and wearing the colors of your school that bind teams together. At the start of each season, I offered sweatshirts and T-shirts for parents to purchase. We offered a navy blue hooded sweatshirt with all of the state championship and conference championship years on the back in gold lettering, something that speaks of tradition. We also offered a T-shirt that had a photo of one of our stars on the front, like Laef Barnes or Evan Garber, a team shot from Nike Cross Nationals, or of Prefontaine. On the back was the schedule or the year-by-year list of Mead's national rankings.

Outfitting the team with uniforms, warm-ups, and other gear requires careful organization. Over time, you will get a feel for the sizes and how many items of each size to order. During the summer, I sent out cards for kids to fill out to indicate their sizes. Meanwhile, I tried to build a relationship with a local silkscreen shop and an apparel sales rep who could give me a good deal. I tried to manage our look with traditional styles that remained constant year after year.

I sold everything at cost. Sweatshirts, stocking caps, and T-shirts weren't items I tried to sell at a profit. To me, it was about getting this stuff into peoples' hands. That way, they became walking billboards for our team.

We generally had 60 to 70 kids on the boys cross country team. Everyone wore the same uniform. The uniform was sacred. I didn't want the guys wearing it any day except meet day. I also kept the same look year after year so that all I had to do was order about a dozen new jerseys and shorts per year to replace the ones that had worn out. I usually cycled uniforms out after five years.

I also shopped at outlet stores to find plain singlets that matched our team colors. I had those screened so that we had alternative jerseys we could break out for a special occasion or wear just for fun. I wanted our traditional bright yellow at the state meet. It became a badge of honor to wear that jersey, a privilege. I encourage any coach to be creative and find the best deal on cool jerseys, and add them to the inventory.

To distribute uniforms, I started with a bunch of plastic bags and made name tags for each one. I sorted the clothes by sizes and figured out how I wanted to distribute the items. Then I took a Sunday afternoon and filled each bag with a jersey, shorts, and warm-ups. Then I placed each bag in the corresponding athlete's locker or handed them out after a practice. That saved time and hassle. The bag I gave out at the start of the season was the same bag I wanted back at the end of the season. In some programs, kids buy their jerseys and keep them when the season is over.

For racing shoes or training shoes, invite someone from your local running store to meet with the team. You can usually get a team discount and a good deal for shoes. Kids need good training shoes and light racing shoes appropriate for the surface they will run on.

Buying the Right Shoes

My college coach Bill Bowerman became famous for more than just coaching runners. He was a cofounder of Nike, and the origins of his business interest was an obsession with shoes. He believed in lightweight shoes, the lighter the better. In college, I and other runners were guinea pigs for the shoes he cobbled together at home.

I encouraged my high school athletes to go to a running shoe specialty store so that they would get better advice on fit and function. Usually, these stores are staffed by runners who know how foot size and shape (e.g., width) and foot strike (heel, midfoot, or ball) affect shoe selection. Athletes should have a training shoe that fits like a glove. These shoes will get dirty and take a beating at times, but the training shoe shouldn't be bulky or heavy. Racing shoes are also important. For cross country, a nonspiked shoe is appropriate on many courses. And a spiked shoe is valuable if you are running on golf courses or other all-grass surfaces or in muddy or snowy conditions.

In a perfect world, a good training shoe, a lightweight road racing flat, and a lightweight track spike should all be in the arsenal. Affordability comes into play for many high school runners, and it is certainly common for them to have only one or two pairs of shoes. Shoe selection for race day is a part of being prepared for a given meet. Test the spike length or other shoe options while previewing the course.

The shoe expert at the running store should be able to help your athletes find the shoes that are right for them based on their foot structure and foot-strike pattern. He or she should also be able to tell them the lifespan of a training shoe. Usually, when shoes lose their bounce, it's time to invest in another pair.

Building a Schedule

When it comes time to determine your meet schedule, the first thing you will do is look at your clientele and make your choices based on that. Do you have a great team? Are you in the middle of the pack? Or are you at ground zero? The last thing you want is to go to a meet and score 1,000 points. You want to find ways to win, and that can be accomplished by picking the right level of competition.

In Spokane, our league meets are placed on the schedule the same way year after year. A coaches' seeding meeting for the following season happens in November. A lottery determines which schools host which meets, such as the district championship, JV championship, and so on. Your meet schedule may be derived in a similar fashion. If your schedule doesn't include dual meets, you have fewer obstacles to work around and a lot more freedom to pick and choose meets. However, the same considerations apply. You don't want to run in a high-intensity meet every weekend. Find meets that are a good match for your talent level so that your athletes can pull something positive out of the experience.

Once I had our league meets in place, I plugged the remaining holes in the calendar with invitational meets. Some of the events we liked to go to were the Stanford Invitational (California), the Richland Invitational (Washington), the Lava Bear Invitational (Bend, Oregon), and the Sunfair Invitational (Yakima, Washington). I found the dates for all of those meets, figured out whether they would work for us, and then went to work nailing them down. For an in-season big invitational such as Stanford, we had to fund-raise to cover the costs of airline tickets. Otherwise, we couldn't go. For premier national meets at the end of the season, Nike Cross Nationals and Foot Locker, meet sponsors cover the travel costs. I never wanted to get stuck a week or two out with some detail that hadn't been addressed.

The talent pool you have should drive your selection of meets. I wouldn't go to Stanford, for instance, if I knew my team couldn't compete for the championship. If dual meets are the focus of your season, find low-key invitationals that will provide you with the racing experience you want. If your team has ambitions to win the league or advance to the state meet, find the meets that match the competitive environment you are looking for. Base your schedule on your culture (see figure 4.1).

I liked to take one overnight trip with the entire team. I picked a meet that was about a two-hour drive from home, brought plenty of chaperones, and made sure safety was a central theme. Parent involvement is huge on overnight trips. I developed a few guidelines for pairing teammates in hotel rooms. Often, I tried to put guys with their best buddy, but it didn't always work out that way. If I had someone who was a bit challenging, I placed him with a team leader that I trusted. I matched varsity runners with other varsity runners, JV with JV, and so on partly because that kept both athletes on the same schedule. If I had a young athlete I felt was an up-and-coming star, I might have put one of my better seniors with him to keep him relaxed and focused. Shadowing a veteran is a valuable way for young runners to gain maturity. It's also important to have one invitational on the schedule that's within a half-hour's drive, so parents, grandparents, and friends can come and see it.

If you have a tough rival or a team that everyone looks at as the big challenge, avoid meeting this team repeatedly during the season. If Mead was ranked No. 1 and Ferris No. 2, and I knew we would have a dual meet against them the last week of the regular season, I wouldn't try to race them at an invitational also. (In a small community like Spokane, all of us coaches knew each other's schedules and who was going where). I'm a mystery guy. I prefer to hide out so the opponent knows less about us. It doesn't always work. Sometimes you have to collide.

Try not to commit to a high-level invitational in September. I learned that lesson the hard way. We went to Vale, Oregon, one year for the Oregon Trail Invitational when we were coming into the season ranked No. 1 nationally. We got slaughtered by Mountain View of Utah. It's tough to have a great day when it's too early, especially when there is a big bull's-eye on your back. Sometimes you don't want people to know what you're holding, or you want to keep them guessing about when you're going to play your cards

---

Figure 4.1   Schedule Planning

Considerations for building a schedule:

- What sort of schedule fits the culture and ability of the team? Try to prepare a schedule that includes the right mix of challenge but also allows the possibility of success.
- Where do the mandatory league dual meets fit and which will be the most challenging?
- Is there an invitational meet that would provide a good overnight experience for everyone on the team?
- Is there a reasonably good local invitational that would allow family and friends to come watch?
- Is there a high-profile meet that you might fly your varsity top seven to?
- Are there teams you would just as soon avoid running against ahead of a big clash?
- Do additional factors or conflicting dates (such as homecoming or college entrance exams) come into play?

and why. I will err on the side of going to an easy invitational early.

In Spokane, there is a randomness to the dual meets, and so it's possible that the three best teams all meet on Sept. 21, and that becomes the Greater Spokane League dual meet championship. It becomes an important date on the schedule and affects which meets to schedule before and after it. I wouldn't take on a challenging invitational meet the week before a dual meet that had championship ramifications.

Each state has limitations on how many competitions a team may enter. In Washington that number is 11. So, with four dates taken by the league dual schedule, plus districts and regionals, 7 of the 11 meets are accounted for. That leaves four more meets for invitationals.

Other factors come into play when figuring out a competition schedule. Maybe gas prices have spiked and it's too expensive to travel far on a bus. Maybe the SAT or ACT college entrance exams are happening on the weekend of a meet you'd like to attend, but it's not in your best interest because half of your top kids need to take the test. The homecoming football game and the dance that usually follows are important to kids on the team. It may not be a good idea to be out of town that day and unable to get back in time for the dance depending on the kids' interests.

Other things will crop up and affect various kids on the team during the course of a season, but generally, they won't require adjusting the schedule.

Building a Coaching Staff

Anyone with head coaching experience understands the value of top-notch assistant coaches. These are the trusted, loyal, capable, vital members of your program. They extend your reach as a coach, help cut down on the endless chores of guiding a team through a season, and amplify your message.

When I got to Mead there was a young assistant coach named Andy Sonneland who had been with the program and the previous head coach. I liked him and retained him.

He knew all of the good places to run in the neighborhood. He knew all the kids' names. And he knew the existing culture. He helped me plug in at Mead until I had gained a footing there. He didn't stay with me long, and when he moved, it was by his own choice. I think anyone moving into a new school or situation would be wise to find someone to help map out the landscape and accelerate the understanding of what's gone on before.

I also brought on the Mead wrestling coach, an enthusiastic and highly motivated character named Cash Stone. He brought excitement and lots of energy, and I loved that about him. He also saw the benefit in getting his wrestlers out for cross country so that they could build their fitness and work ethic through the fall. That was music to my ears.

The first year I was at Mead, one of the wrestlers cracked our top seven. We had about 20 wrestlers on the team that fall and that helped with numbers as I worked to establish my vision of the program. Three years after I started at Mead, we started winning championships and some of those wrestlers were valuable depth guys. And they were almost always hard workers. Cash was involved with the cross country team for about eight years. He was a good recruiter, he was good at equipment inventory, and he was a positive person. That positivity is a key point when you are putting together a staff. You want to be surrounded by people who are positive and who love working with kids.

There is a second key type of coach. This is someone who can work out with the kids, keep them honest out on runs, and also keep everyone accounted for. I used to do that in my early days at Mead, but when guys started beating me, I knew I needed to find someone else, and then I found Scott Daratha. Over the years, I found that most of the coaches in the Spokane area wanted an assistant like Scott, someone who was respected as a runner. For any cross country program, it's a great asset.

Cash and Scott were always involved in our Monday pizza nights, they were involved in our morning runs, and they were involved in our weekend and overnight trips. They could also handle our warm-up exercises. Your assistant coaches give you the opportunity

Scott Daratha

As I began to get a little too old to lead my best guys on runs, I came to the realization that I should delegate that responsibility to an assistant. That's where Scott Daratha came in. He was one of the better road racers in the Spokane area and a Mead graduate.

Scott could take the kids on runs and keep the tempo sweet. I think it's important to have a younger runner as an assistant coach. This person can serve as an example for proper running form and mechanics, proper attitude, and the lifestyle we are aiming for. It's important to have someone with active running credentials on staff, someone the kids can see and work with every day.

Not only was Scott a loyal assistant who never questioned my approach to coaching, but he also had the kids' respect and trust as a runner. In Scott, we had a perfect example of someone who brought valued skills to our program, and we used his strengths. Today, Scott is a head cross country coach at Deer Park High School, north of Spokane.

to focus on other things. Cash and Scott and other assistants I had along the way at Mead understood their roles. And I always tried to pay them their due respect at our awards night at the conclusion of the season.

Whomever you choose as an assistant has to be loyal to you and respect that you are the boss. Defining the rules and responsibilities for each coach is important. When Scott was an assistant coach, his responsibilities started in the summer. He was around on most of our workout session days while I was often away at various running camps. He also took charge during Christmas vacation when I took my annual vacation. During the season, Scott usually warmed up the kids, and he took our high-end athletes on runs, tempos, and fartleks and kept them focused. He had a role in distributing uniforms, setting up the awards night, chaperoning trips, and performing room checks.

Cash's primary duties were distributing uniforms (and collecting them), setting up our team area at all competitions, making sure we

had all the water and ice we needed, washing all of the towels in our locker room, and helping set up and take down the course when we hosted meets. He was also an inspirational person, so he always led a cheer on the starting line before the race. And he also had one unusual talent that we liked to put to good use. He could yodel. So when the moment called for it, he yodeled to help celebrate a kid's performance.

I had another volunteer assistant who loved computer work and logistics. He was ideal for keeping our inventory of uniforms and other gear on a spreadsheet, and I could count on him to pick up packets at meet sites and distribute numbers or race bibs to the athletes. He also liked to create newsletters and put together our team rulebook. I was our team photographer, but that is a role that many coaches delegate to an assistant coach or parent.

Here are a couple of key points to consider when forming a staff:

- **Avoid redundancy.** Sometimes you will have people with overlapping skills and interests, but as a rule you don't want two assistant coaches doing the same broad sweep of duties. It is better to make each one responsible for specific roles.

- **Surround yourself with positive people.** Not only is this something that will help the morale of the team, but also it will reduce the stresses that come with coaching.

- **Find a runner.** Kids respond positively to an assistant coach who has running credibility and brings racing experience and successful habits to the table.

- **Look for a charismatic character.** Someone on the staff needs to be an energetic recruiter and create a buzz that attracts students to come out for the team, particularly if he or she is amplifying your message. It's also important that this person be loyal to your vision.

- **Play to strengths.** If you have an assistant coach who has advanced organizational skills, delegate jobs that are appropriate and interesting to that coach. Ask your coaches what they want to do and tailor roles that fit them.

- **Don't be afraid to cut someone loose.** Passion for helping only goes so far. If an assistant coach isn't making a positive contribution to the team or is disloyal to your vision as the head coach, it will only drag the program down. It's better to relieve that coach of his or her duties than to let a bad situation fester.

- **Praise your assistants for their effort.** Just because your assistant coaches are adults doesn't mean they don't respond to praise or appreciate a thank-you for their work. Assistant coaches work long hours for minimal financial gain because they love what they're doing and they love the kids. Always keep in mind that you are in this process together.

My Coaching Start

In 1983, my first fall coaching at Shorecrest High School, I inherited a pretty good group, but nobody on the team was exceptional. There were a few 10:00 two-milers in the lineup. They were guys who had some short-comings on the track but were pretty good in cross country. I got a little more out of them, and we qualified for the state championship and placed third. At this time in Washington, the benchmark in the state was Edmonds High, coached by Tom Campbell and our neighbor. In 1984 and 1985, we won back-to-back state titles. The last one was special for me because it was at Hangman Valley in Spokane, the site of Prefontaine's last race in an Oregon jersey.

Those first few years in high school, I tried to use my magic by being enthusiastic and promoting the values that I had studied from legends like UCLA basketball coach John Wooden, such as industriousness, friend-ship, and loyalty, which come straight from his Pyramid of Success. I was into creating music mixes and theme songs for the team, and I used Queen's "We Are The Champions." The kids assembled in the gym, and they closed their eyes as we listened to it and walked through their race plan for state.

The things I did at Shorecrest were the things I'd learned at Oregon. And I took that same formula to Mead. The night that the movie *Marathon Man,* starring Dustin Hoffman, came out, I got my team together at Green Lake Park, and we ran the four or five miles (6.4 or 8 km) into downtown Seattle for the premiere.

Building Mead Into a Winner: 1986-1990

It didn't take long to figure out that I was onto something special at Mead. Right away, the team ran some really good workouts that first fall, and the guys were already in the habit of morning runs before school. In 1987, we fin-ished with a dual record of 6-2, but we didn't get the break we needed at the regional meet and placed fourth. Only the top two teams qualified for state, and we were beaten by three very good teams. But that season was about creating momentum. We may have missed qualifying as a team, but Chris Lewis salvaged our season by going to state as an individual and winning the race.

Motivated by the pain of not qualifying for the state meet, the guys on the team dedi-cated themselves to making sure that didn't happen again. We established a high-quality group behind Chris Lewis that included Nathan Davis, Yukon Degenhart, and Greg Kuntz. The 1988 team was one of the best the state had seen to that point, with three guys under 15:00 for three miles at the state meet and six of the seven under 16:00. We scored 43 points for a new low-score record at the state meet. What was so cool about that experience was that nobody had been to state before in that group except for Lewis.

For the most part, the 1988 team didn't have any doubt. I could see it in their eyes. That team already believed it could fly. The guys were excited. Lewis was a phenomenal leader and inspired the other guys on the team by doing things in workouts that caused them to say, "Whoa!" A sports writer in Spo-kane said that Lewis "looked like an altar boy

Chris Lewis (417) was a two-time state champion in Washington and helped set the bar for the runners who came up after him at Mead.

and ran like the devil." We ate that up. They all knew he'd be our "low stick" and score one point. Lewis brought energy.

In Spokane, running was popular and you could read about Lewis. I played that up. Lewis had a bounce. He was a high-toe runner, very graceful to watch. He also bought into the stories I told him about Pre, and the other guys did too. Lewis didn't like to lose. He was a risk taker and a front-runner. When he was a sophomore, I could still beat him when we went out on training runs. By the time he was a junior, he was the first guy back and was beating me. As a senior, he ran the fastest 1,600 meters (4:04) and 3,200 meters (8:50) in the country during track season and made *Sports Illustrated*'s "Faces in the Crowd" column.

The challenge in 1989 was to see whether we could win the state championship again, but this time without Lewis, who had graduated after his second-straight individual title. The guys we brought back all got better. Kuntz and Davis, the two seniors, led the way. Kuntz began as a timid, shy kid who turned into something special. He won the state title, Davis was third, and we won the team title again, this time with 41 points

and again breaking the record. We also were ranked third nationally in Marc Bloom's *Harrier Magazine*.

The wheels were turning, the commitment to summer training increased, and expectations continued to grow. We were shadowing excellence, and we didn't have to look outside the program to find it. Our younger runners were modeling themselves after the seniors. But there were also challenges along the way. In 1988, one of our top guys was killed in an auto accident. Any time something tragic like that happens, it's a devastating blow to the cross country family and a stark reminder about what's important. But when you build meaning into your running, it simply doesn't stop. We dedicated our season to the memory of Matthew Zweifel.

In 1990, we were at a summer camp in Clear Lake, high up on White Pass in the Cascade Mountains. We ran up the slope of a mountain to the top of a chairlift, which we would use to come back down. The Mead guys were the first to the top of the run and the first to board the chairlift. I was about six rows back from the front, and the chairs were filled one after another. Because the chairs going up were empty and there were about 10 rows filled going down, the lift got out of balance and we began to accelerate to the bottom of the hill.

It was a scary ride on a runaway chairlift that got even worse when the seats snapped off at the bottom of the hill and threw everyone onto the ground. Matt Davis, a promising eighth-grader, got beat up pretty bad, breaking an ankle, an arm, and a couple of teeth. The eighth-grader seated next to him, Doug Morse, broke his femur. They got the worst of it. Others were able to run off at the platform but had no place to go except into a pile of bodies. The lift stopped and that left people stranded, dangling above the ground for an hour and a half. I felt terrible and tried to calm everyone, but it was an ugly situation.

After something like that, all you can do is stand up and get back together and move on. We were lucky that time. Later that fall, with three of the top seven back, we managed to win the state championship again. Led by seniors Degenhart and Erik Johnson placing fourth and seventh, respectively, we won easily with 43 points.

That team had marvelous unity, and at least some of that had to stem from what we'd been through on that mountain—their toughness. Erik Johnson was a natural leader. Yukon Degenhart's dad had been a mining engineer up in Alaska. That's how he came by the nickname Yukon, and his name was so cool he became one of our icons.

Maintaining the Mead Dynasty: 1991-1996

Mead won its third-straight Washington Interscholastic Activities Association state championship in the fall of 1990, placing five runners in the top 20, but there was more going on at that meet than most people realized.

A trio of ninth-graders, still in junior high, took part in a fun run at the conclusion of the state meet. Right up in the front of that race were Matt Davis, Rob Aubrey, and Greg James. All three were buddies. All three were from Spokane. And all three were headed to Mead to reload the school's fabled cross country program in another nine months.

Davis, Aubrey, and James had grown up playing soccer together. Matt Davis and his little brother Micah had watched their older brother Nathan win state titles on Mead's 1988 and 1989 teams.

In the summer of 1991, the talented sophomore class arrived. Matt Davis became the runner that most approximated the tenacity and spirit of Prefontaine in all my years at Mead. Aubrey, James, Skiy DeTray, Barry Morig, and Micah Davis became the central characters of the team. These guys loved each other. They ran with passion and courage. They worked hard and had fun.

The top five from 1990 all graduated, but we got better in 1991 with the young guys. Matt Davis won the state title, running 14:48 for three miles. Morig, a junior, was second, and Chris Phillips was a huge surprise at fifth. He had been our fifth man at the regional qualifying meet. The 1991 team scored 28 points to break the all-time low-score record by 13 (set by the 1989 team).

In 1992, all seven of the runners we took to state placed in the top 17, and we broke the meet scoring record again, this time with 20 points. Davis won his second straight title, Morig was fourth, Aubrey was fifth, and sophomore Micah Davis was seventh. Second-place Richland finished 110 points behind us. Davis had gotten very strong. He stayed with the front pack for about a mile (1.6 km) and then tore off in the second mile. No one could cover that second-mile surge. As an added bonus, at the conclusion of the season *Harrier Magazine* rated us the No. 1 team in the United States. And we all knew that we hadn't reached our peak yet.

We entered the 1993 season as preseason No. 1 in the country with five great guys back and a lot of expectations. It was a team of high school runner rock stars and we loved that.

But on Sept. 10, on a hot, dry, dusty day in Vale, Oregon, the Mead machine hit a brick wall. It was the Oregon Trail Invitational, and we showed up looking to take care of business without Matt Davis in the lineup because he was nursing a sore knee. Mountain View of Orem, Utah, scored 30 points. We finished with 97. Aubrey finished third, Micah Davis

The 1991 Mead team scored a record-low 28 points to win the state championship. One year later, they broke their own record when they scored 20 points with Matt Davis leading the way.

was sixth, Skiy DeTray was eighth. But then we dropped off to 35th and 45th.

We were stunned. It was our first loss in six years. That night, we slept on the gym floor at Vale High School along with a bunch of other teams. But I couldn't sleep, and none of the other guys could sleep either. At midnight, I whispered to everyone to follow me outside and into the parking lot. Everyone gathered in a circle and I spoke, "Gang, we need to get this off our chest right now. It feels like somebody died. Nobody died. We got beat. Now it's time to move on." We did some soul searching out in that parking lot. We dealt with the loss right then, sat and talked about it, and then went back into the gym and went to sleep.

When we returned to Spokane the next day, you could sense that the gravity of the loss had taken a toll and also strengthened the group's resolve. The guys wanted another chance to be ranked No. 1 in the nation. Three weeks later, at the Sunfair Invitational in Yakima, Washington, we achieved a perfect score by winning all seven flighted races (in each race a single varsity runner from each team

competed against his counterpart from all the other teams. All the No. 1s raced each other, and the No. 2s raced each other, and so on.).

Motivated by the loss in Vale, the guys came to practice every day focused and unwilling to allow mental lapses or let anything interfere with the team goals. Obviously, the return of Matt Davis, our leader and best runner, made a big difference. Davis in particular was determined to do everything the right way. After Sunfair, we took on North Central High School in a GSL meet and won with a perfect score of 15-50. Our guys moved over the course like a flock of geese. Davis crossed the finish line first, but our other six guys were within a second of him. We scored 58 points and rolled to victory at the Richland Invitational. And then we came back home and beat a pretty good Ferris team 17-45.

At the state championship, Davis became the first runner in Washington history to win three consecutive titles, and he won by 37 seconds in a new course record of 14:09.3. Behind him, his brother Micah (14:46) was second, Rob Aubrey (14:48) was third, and

Greg James was eighth (15:13). We scored 31 points for our sixth title in a row.

To reclaim the No. 1 national ranking we had to go to the Foot Locker West Regional meet and do something special there. We were feeling full of confidence.

At the Foot Locker regional, our brains were tuned into running as well as we could as a team with the additional hope of getting a couple guys qualified for the national individual finals in San Diego. The guys ran better than they had at state. On the California state meet course at Woodward Park in Fresno, Matt Davis won the regional race and beat future Olympic medalist Meb Keflezighi. Micah Davis was eighth, Rob Aubrey was 16th, Greg James was 43rd, and Skiy DeTray was 67th.

The result was that our top five runners scored the fastest combined time over the Woodward Park course and set a record that would stand for a long time. Arcadia of California only recently broke that record. Mountain View of Utah was also there, and we turned the tables on the result from September. In the wake of the Foot Locker West Regional, Mead moved back to No. 1 in the country.

The 1993 season was the pinnacle of a 20-year run at Mead, and I think it's fairly regarded as one of the great teams in the history of U.S. high school cross country. It had some great characters. The senior leader, Matt Davis, had the whole package: mind, body, and most emphatically, spirit. Nobody could sneak past him. He never stopped looking over his shoulder or took for granted that he was better than the next guy. He was also all about the team. Davis was the only guy in state history to go three for three at the championship meet, and he wrapped it up by placing third at the 1993 Foot Locker national final. Everyone came in each day ready to compete, for the most part they didn't get hurt, and they were good at communicating if they were feeling discomfort.

The 1994 team fed off that success and kept the ball rolling, but it also had to work for it. There was a moment when the dynasty teetered on the brink. At our regional meet that year, only the winner qualified to the state championship. We had to rally in the final half mile to beat Ferris 35 points to 38 to lock up that berth. It was a powerful challenge from a hungry Ferris team, and we barely managed to fend it off. At state, Micah Davis picked up where his brother had left off and won the state title; Skiy DeTray was fourth. We won the championship with 46 points and were ranked No. 7 nationally.

We graduated our top three and number five from the 1994 state meet team. But as the last of the three Davis brothers left the program, another family was just getting started. In 1995, we had a new front-runner named Jason Fayant. He was third at the state meet, Morgan Thompson was seventh, and Mead finished on top for the eighth year in a row.

In 1996, we had a nice deep team. Ryan Wiser and Fayant finished seventh and eighth, respectively. Thompson and Chad Wiser were 17th and 18th. We scored 34 points and ran the streak of state championships to nine in a row. We had managed to make winning a habit, but I don't think we ever got complacent about it. There were always new challenges on the horizon.

Summary

It takes a thoughtful, organized approach to build a program. Pay attention to the details, make smart choices, and always try to prepare as early as possible.

- Recruiting students who are likely to fit into your program is one of the most important roles of a cross country coach. Sell the sport by spreading the word about the aspects of the program that kids find cool, such as trips, winning, and school spirit.
- Plan how you will organize and distribute team gear, because how kids look is important to them.
- Prepare a schedule that is in sync with the abilities of your team. Enter meets that give your team an appropriate competitive challenge.
- Assemble a coaching staff that is loyal to you and offers a variety of skills that will help you cover all of your bases.

PART II

PLANNING AND TRAINING

CHAPTER 5

Planning for the Season

Commitment to cross country begins with the idea that running is a year-round sport. It's an everyday activity that you incorporate into your life, like brushing your teeth. Successful cross country seasons are not forged in the two and a half months before the state championships. They are the product of summer training, spring track and field, and winter training.

There are no days off in the ongoing process of becoming a better runner. This is what I learned in high school, and it was also my experience in college. That's why for the most committed runners, it is a lifestyle choice. There is a rhythm to it, day by day, week by week, and season by season. That is also how you build a cardiorespiratory base and a capacity for work that grows over time.

Here we delve into year-round training and the principles that guide that training and also map out the week-by-week workouts that complement the competitive fall cross country season.

Running: A Year-Round Sport

Depending on where you live, the formal coaching of runners in U.S. high schools could last from early March to the first week of June for track season. In the East, where indoor track is most popular, cross country season bleeds into winter indoor and then outdoor track in the spring. And cross country usually picks up in mid-August and lasts to early November. For a select few athletes, the cross country season extends to December and national championship meets.

In Washington, the seasons leave a gap in the winter and summer. I never planned those in-between months, but I encouraged my athletes to run every day for at least an hour. That's a reasonable goal, and it goes back to making a lifestyle choice. If you are committed to being a runner, going out for an hour a day isn't a burden. It's just part of the daily routine.

For top teams, the cross country season can extend into the first weekend of December for the Nike Cross Nationals, meaning runners need to be prepared for cold weather.

For high school programs, rules often limit organized training during the off-season. Usually, a team is allowed to do conditioning together, but coaches aren't allowed to organize a workout and go out to the track. There were never rules about getting into a car and going out to some cool running trails, and so we did that. In the winter, it gets darker earlier and the weather gets tougher, especially in the Northwest. I encouraged the kids to get in a couple of road races during the winter months.

During the summer, you can continue to aim for an hour a day. The quality of that hour depends largely on the individual drive and talent of the athlete. When I began at Mead, we tried to meet three days a week. We avoided the heat of the day, and an earlier start time of 9:00 a.m. provided more structure to the kids' mornings. The other four days of the week were optional, and a smaller, more dedicated group would usually make it.

Particularly in the summer, it's a good idea to change the scenery. We took short road trips out of town to find trails that were out of our range during the typical school week. I also encouraged kids to attend summer running camps. I took about a dozen or so to the University of Oregon camp every summer.

Take time in the summer not only to train and cover new ground, but also to explore your area's running heritage. Find out where your local legends grew up and identify where they ran. Take your kids to those spots, soak up that history, and use it for inspiration. It's even better if that runner is still around and can come and meet your team and tell his or her story.

No matter whether we were in the doldrums of winter training or the heat of the summer, we still met like a club. We still held the pizza gathering every Monday. Even though competitive seasons may vary on the calendar and leave gaps in the winter and summer, it's important to maintain year-round continuity. Running has two seasons in a calendar year, but it is a 365-day effort. Every component of training, from winter to spring to summer to fall is connected.

Five Principles of the Oregon System

Back in the 1920s, the world saw the rise of the first great distance runner, a Finnish athlete named Paavo Nurmi. He was one of the first middle- and long-distance racers to devise a system of training that had serious thought behind it. He ran almost everywhere—in training and in races—with a stopwatch in his hand. It was the precursor to interval training. The Swedish term *fartlek* came along in the late 1930s, referring to speed play built into training runs. In the 1950s and 1960s iconic coaches Percy Cerutty (Australia) and Arthur Lydiard (New Zealand) opened new horizons for runners with their ideas about how to take training to new levels. Cerutty experimented with a holistic lifestyle that included hard training in natural surroundings. He was into developing the mind as well as the body and outlined strict rules governing things such as diet. Lydiard came along and applied the science of base training to build endurance and then added periodization to it, precepts that almost every coach in the world follows today.

Bill Bowerman at the University of Oregon was also influential in the evolution of training methods in the 1960s. He traveled to New Zealand and befriended Lydiard and brought the principals of jogging back to the United States. At the same time, Bowerman was coaching some of America's pioneering sub-4:00 milers like Jim Bailey, Dyrol Burleson, and Jim Grelle. His first great distance runner, Bill Dellinger, competed in three Olympics and won the bronze medal in the 5,000 meters at the 1964 Tokyo Games. Bowerman took what he learned and, along with Dellinger, established the Oregon system.

These are the five principles that inform every decision I make about training my athletes: moderation, progression, variation, adaptation, and callousing. These informed the training of Steve Prefontaine, Rudy Chapa, Bill McChesney, Alberto Salazar, Galen Rupp, and many others. Here is a closer look at each one.

Moderation

Bill Bowerman always used to say, "Train, don't strain." Rest is just as important as intensity and is necessary to create balance in training. Taken a step further, moderation should exist in just about every aspect of a runner's life. This includes eating habits, television and video game consumption, and just about anything else that knocks a balanced life out of kilter.

Moderation as it applies to the Oregon system of training means developing a rhythm consisting of two hard days during the week, a third day that is a little less difficult, one day for a long run, and three days that are easy recovery. Bowerman always said to err on the side of too little work rather than too much overall. One of the great challenges of coaching is finding the line between too much and too little and then knowing how to stay on the conservative side of it. Rhythm and a balance go into writing workouts.

Left to their own devices, most runners would not only flirt with that line but cross over it and do too much. Alberto Salazar, who came along at Oregon after I did and became one of the world's greatest marathoners, would no doubt agree with this. His career ended too soon because he did too much work and didn't allow himself enough rest. It is the coach's responsibility to respect that balance and to know better. Otherwise, athletes will get injured.

Progression

To get faster or to build endurance, a runner has to progress. Any runner, especially a young runner, wants to achieve new personal bests every year. You and your runners also want to be able to measure the progression that happens during the course of a season, from one competition to the next. It's the improvement over time and the steps taken in training to achieve that improvement that is important.

For instance, an eighth-grader who is involved in a running program for the first time might run 30 to 40 miles (48-64 km) per week. Two years later, as a 10th-grader, the runner's mileage might go up to 50 to 60 miles (80-97 km) per week. As a senior, that same runner may be up to 70 miles (112 km) per week or a little more. At Mead, our top guns ran right about 70 miles per week.

We would build up to these totals in the off season and sustain them into the early season. As the season progressed, we would taper to less. If our top runners were running 70 miles per week in the early season, they would gradually decrease to running only 40 miles a week prior to the state meet.

Progression should come gradually. I always thought that a freshman boy who could run between 4:40 and 4:50 for the mile could be very good by the time he graduated high school. I found that sophomore year was usually a big indicator of how that might turn out based on how quickly the runner was maturing physically. Beyond those issues, quality training makes a significant difference in progression. Intense workouts that incorporate date-pace and goal-pace intervals are important components of the second principle. (Determining date pace and goal pace are explained in chapter 8.) Date pace is the pace you run currently for your race distance, and goal pace is the pace you want to achieve at the end of the season. Progression also means addressing weaknesses related to posture and proper running form, habits that can be corrected by exercises to build strength and instruction to improve mechanics.

Variation

Variety is not only the spice of life. It's also the spice of training, and without variation, it can start to become stale. A variety of training elements should include tempo runs, fartleks, intervals, easy days, running in the forest, running on the track, running on the roads, and so on. As a coach, you have to mix things up to keep training interesting.

At Mead, I was lucky. In the neighborhoods surrounding the school, there were hills when we wanted hills, flat when we wanted flat, trails, roads, and grass, and we used all of it. Two or three days a week we went to interesting places not far from school.

We even ran a half-mile stretch of the Little Spokane River. It was a little slippery but not very deep. We finished that run by climbing an S-curve up and out of the river and back to Mead, where we did 12 × 100-meter strides on the grass, barefoot.

About 10 loops comprised our most common places to run, and they contained a lot of variety. We used them during the spring track season, too. In the middle of April, I might have noticed that a particular kid, or the whole group, was in a rut. My response to that was to go back to our roots, back to the trails and run fartleks and play games. Sometimes you need to put energy back in your life, and that's what gets a kid back to feeling frisky again.

Adaptation

Sometimes it takes creativity to stay on task or to overcome adverse training conditions. What if you don't have a track at your school? What if you have a track, but it's covered by snow? What if you live in an area that's flat as a pancake and you want to run hills?

Adaptation is the art of making things work even when obstacles get in the way. I can tell you that it was quite often so windy or rainy at the Mead High School track in the spring that I timed just 50 percent of our intervals. Sometimes, you have to put the watch away and run with heart. We'd just go into what I called Rocky mode, running on guts and emotion. If you don't have hills, find a parking garage, stairs, or bridges.

My mentor Bill Dellinger didn't have a track to train on when he was serving in the Air Force before the 1960 Rome Games. He was stationed at a remote radar station on Washington's Olympic Peninsula. So he went to the beach near Port Angeles and counted off the number of strides it took for him to run 400 meters. While he was serving in the Air Force, in 1958, he set an American record in the 1,500 meters.

The point of adaptation is to figure out how to maintain your training goals even when conditions aren't perfect. For example, if you are scheduled to do a three × 1,600-meter workout at 5:00 pace and a snowstorm covers the track, find a way to adapt. Do that workout on a passable road. Or do it on a treadmill.

Callousing

There is great value in mental toughness and being prepared to handle any situation. A calloused runner doesn't wilt from race conditions that are too hot, doesn't gasp on courses at elevation, and doesn't get flustered when a shoe comes off in the middle of the race. Runners have to be ready to face anything on meet day and handle it with a "no sweat" attitude.

If you are going to race in the heat, then sometimes you have train in the heat. If you are flying across the country for a race that begins at 10:00 a.m. and that's 7:00 a.m. in your time zone, then it's wise to do some workouts at 7:00 a.m. If you are going to race at altitude, you have to find a way to simulate it beforehand. At Oregon, Coach Dellinger would help us simulate altitude by having us perform a fartlek while holding our breath for an interval of time. He would place cones around a field with signs on each one: easy jog, gradual pickup, hold your breath, and finishing race pace. Ultimately, it is important to prepare athletes by creating workouts that simulate the conditions of the race. You can also callous your runners to respond to surges at different stages of a race so that they are ready for every possibility.

Another issue is falling. Sometimes it happens early in a congested race or even later navigating a slippery corner or slope. Practice what to do after a fall so that your runner doesn't feel sorry for himself or herself and lose focus. Callousing is about preparing to compete well and feeling confident that nothing stands in the way of achieving the race plan. This is mental conditioning.

Do intervals in the wind to get used to having a breeze in your face during a competition. Run wearing two or three layers of sweats to simulate heat. When I was in college, coach Dellinger made us jog in place in a sauna in order to get ready for the NCAA Championships in Baton Rouge, Louisiana. He wanted us to know what it felt like, and worse, before we got off the plane in Louisiana and felt the heat and humidity.

The longer you coach, the greater the likelihood that you will have an athlete deal with a tragedy or adversity. A family member dies. Parents divorce. A pet dies. As a coach, you

Courtesy of Price Photography

Callousing involves learning how to deal with variables that are uncomfortable, like hot weather, or unusual, like an unfamiliar trail, and being mentally capable of pushing through them.

Forgotten Shoes

Micah Davis was usually organized and ready to go, but the day we arrived in Fresno for the Foot Locker West Regional Cross Country Championships, he realized he'd made a mistake.

He had left his racing shoes in Spokane. There was not enough time to ship them. When he came to me with the news of the missing shoes, I rolled with it. I didn't want anything to upset Micah in his preparation for the race. I asked a couple of other coaches I knew who had athletes in the race whether they had an extra pair of shoes and told them Micah's size. Lo and behold, one of the athletes had a spare pair and was happy to loan them to Micah.

The fit wasn't perfect, but Micah focused on the good in the situation. He had shoes to wear and they served him well in the race. The important thing was he didn't freak out about it. He qualified for nationals and a week later finished 10th in the championship race.

can let your kids know there will be hardships in life and that quite often, running is an escape from loss or other difficult times. They can dedicate their effort to someone they are thinking about. In my case, I always had the loss of my friend Prefontaine to dedicate effort to.

A few years after I started coaching in a Seattle-area middle school, a boy on my cross country team went home one day after practice, got into an argument with a parent, and shot himself. News of the suicide was a crushing blow to the community. I was devastated and so was everyone associated with the team, and we mourned and let the grief out. But we didn't stop running.

Organizing a Time Trial

At some point before the first meet of the season you'll want to establish who the fastest seven athletes on the team are, and the best way to do it is through a competition that simulates the real thing. Time trials come in all shapes and sizes, and establishing a method that is fair is important to the athletes. These intrasquad competitions can be intense, emotional moments for members of the team who are on the cusp of making the varsity.

I've used several options for time trials, and I generally prefer that additional runners be involved. So we held an alumni event on our home course over Labor Day weekend. A couple of times I invited an outside team to come and take part. That way, there is a team component to focus on in addition to the time trial. I've also held an hourlong run, which we dubbed the Full-Moon Twilight to establish our top seven.

The purpose of a time trial is more than establishing a pecking order, however. Usually, little is revealed in that respect that you don't already know from monitoring day-to-day workouts. Instead, time trials are about rehearsing to compete. They get early-season butterflies out of the system and create initial buzz around your team to start the season. As a coach, you can use the data you collect from a time trial to gauge what kind of season you expect to have. If you have been at it a few years and have held time trials in the same fashion, you can compare one year's time trial to the next. The results of the time trial can also determine which athletes belong in which workout groups, because they are usually an accurate measure of fitness.

Coming out of a time trial, you should have a reasonably secure handle on who is in the top seven, the B group (next seven), and so forth. Opportunities should exist to move up from one group to the next so that your athletes remain motivated to improve, but the first time trial of the season should, at the least, tell you what to expect in the first meet of the season.

Writing Workouts

I followed the practice of my college coach Bill Dellinger, who posted the weekly workout schedule on Monday morning in the locker room. That way, everybody on the team could look at the plan and know what to expect.

I always thought that system worked well. I posted the weekly schedule in the locker room or in my classroom, and the kids knew what we were going to do for the whole week. I always maintained a coach's option to call an audible and make an adjustment on the fly.

Here are the weekly instructions I posted each Monday morning for my team at Mead in the late summer and fall of 2005. The contents of this 11-week plan are closely aligned to the previous 19 years' worth of cross country season workouts.

WEEK 1

Monday	Easy 50-60 minute run, followed by stretching, gut-busters, and push-ups (SGP)
Tuesday	6 × water tower, downhill on Fairwood, hit the S-curves hard, and then jog back to Mead, plus SGP
Wednesday	Recovery day, 40- to 60-minute jog, plus SGP
Thursday	Fartlek over Mead's grass fields, 30 minutes, plus SGP
Friday	River Run, plus 12 × grass strides, plus SGP
Saturday	Indian Painted Rocks fartlek
Sunday	60- to 90-minute run

Notes: The acronym SGP refers to stretching, gut-busters (abdominal work), and push-ups. During the season, we do this routine (outlined in more detail in chapter 6) Monday through Friday. The stretching routine lasts about 10 minutes, the abdominal and core exercises last 5 to 10 minutes, and we wrap it up with push-ups, usually 50. The end of the workout is a great time for this important work, and it's also an opportunity to give the workout some closure, comment on it, and remind the athletes what's coming the next day.

The water tower is a landmark that is part of an 800-meter loop that contains hills. We do it six times with a 90-second recovery between, and we typically alternate directions. Following that, we go on a light jog through the neighborhoods, down a steep hill, and then up a steep S-curve to Mead. The pace for the intervals is current cross country race pace, or what we call date pace.

Fartlek, or speed play, is a cornerstone of cross country training, and there is more about it in chapter 6. We use many variations.

The River Run is something that evolved into a tradition. We found something really cool that I'm not sure any other cross country team has. It was in our area and we used it. The Little Spokane River is about a mile from the school. We run to it, descend a steep bank, and run in the slow-moving current for about 20 minutes, having a blast on a hot summer day. The guys bring old running shoes on Fridays, which is the only day we do this one. Then we run back, hitting that same uphill S-curve. And when we return to school, we do 12 strides on the football field, end line to end line (110 m). And we do these barefoot, each repeat a little faster than the previous one.

Indian Painted Rocks is a park with interesting trails, and yes, there are Native American hieroglyphs there. This was a short road trip we used to break up the monotony. It's an eight-mile loop (13 km) with occasional steepness. We hit the uphills hard and the downhills easy, and because it was a narrow track, we ran single file. My car was usually filled with water and bagels so that everyone could have a drink and a bite to eat.

> *continued*

> continued

WEEK 2

Monday	9 a.m., 50- to 60-minute run, plus SGP
Tuesday	3 p.m., 5 × 1,000 meters with 200-meter recovery drill on track, plus SGP
Wednesday	3 p.m., 50- to 60-minute run, plus SGP (parent meeting at 6 p.m.)
Thursday	3 p.m., Oregon drill, 30 minutes, plus SGP
Friday	9 a.m., River Run plus 12 strides on grass, plus SGP
Saturday	9 a.m., time trial (top finishers qualify for Stanford trip)
Sunday	60- to 90-minute run

Notes: The intervals on Tuesday are held on the track and performed at date pace.

The Oregon drill takes 30 minutes and is run barefoot on the grass of the football or soccer field. I set up cones on each goal line. The cones designate three lanes: one for easy pace, one for medium pace, and one for closing-speed pace. There is a light jog recovery between these strides and the drill runs for a solid 30 minutes, moving from one lane to the next continuously (see chapter 7).

The time trial is a standard 5,000-meter race on our home course. Ideally, I tried to arrange it in conjunction with an alumni meet, but holding it on Labor Day weekend proved difficult over the years to schedule the alumni meet.

WEEK 3

Monday	Labor Day, 40 to 50 minutes easy, plus SGP
Tuesday	Morning: light 20 to 30 minutes Afternoon: two-man 300-meter relay, 12 × hill, plus SGP
Wednesday	Morning: long loop Afternoon: 6- to 7-mile (9.6-11 km) loop on soft surface (40-50 minutes), plus SGP
Thursday	Fartlek on grass (5-4-3-2-1), plus SGP
Friday	River Run plus 12 grass strides, plus SGP
Saturday	9 a.m., road trip to Seven Mile course, 2-1-30 fartlek
Sunday	60- to 90-minute run

Notes: Tuesday marked the first day of the school year. It was usually 90 degrees, and by the afternoon everyone was tired. We didn't need a lot of organization on the first day, so we jogged to a shady park called Brentwood. We divided the team into two-man relay teams. Each runner crossed the flat park, about 300 meters, and slapped hands with his partner, who took off the other way. While waiting, each runner jogged in place during recovery. Then we usually did something else, such as run hills before heading back to school. I had Popsicles in the freezer if it was a hot day.

Thursday's fartlek (5-4-3-2-1) was held in a park or on the school grounds. It consisted of a five-minute surge followed by four minutes easy, four-minute surge, three minutes easy, three-minute surge, and so on. If it was a hot day, I sometimes turned the sprinkler system on.

Seven Mile is a nice trail area. We'd do four or five sets of two-minute surge, two minutes easy, one-minute surge, one minute easy, 30-second surge, 30 seconds easy (2-1-30). This is also called the Don Kardong fartlek.

WEEK 4

Monday	Morning: long loop
	Afternoon: bus departs at 2:50 for Cheney for single file, plus SGP
Tuesday	Morning: long loop
	Afternoon: relaxing 40- to 50-minute run, plus SGP
Wednesday	Morning: light, short loop
	Afternoon: out of class at 2 p.m., bus departs at 2:20 p.m. to Cheney for meet with Shadle Park and University High
Thursday	Morning: long loop
	Afternoon: 20- to 30-minute run, plus 500-400-300-200-100 and cool-down, plus SGP
Friday	Morning: short loop
	Afternoon: bus departs at 2:50 p.m. to Shadle Park for easy course jog
Saturday	8 a.m., bus departs to Shadle Park Invitational
Sunday	Easy 60- to 90-minute run

Notes: Our district was generous about letting us have buses so we could preview courses. I did this one and sometimes two days before a meet. In this case, we went on a Monday to prepare for a Wednesday meet. For the single file, we divided the team into groups of five or six and ran a fartlek over the course. The leader dictated the pace and each member of the group circulated up to the front.

Because we had an invitational on Saturday, the challenge was in keeping our training on track while running two meets in four days. What we did the day after the Wednesday meet was go for an easy run and then go to the track. This workout was a 500-meter stride, a 400-meter jog, a 400-meter stride, a 300-meter jog, a 300-meter stride, and so on. Begin the workout at the start of the backstretch (300 meters from finish), and the workout will conclude with 100s that end at the finish line. I didn't worry about timing the strides, but just wanted them to be crisp.

WEEK 5

Monday	Morning: long loop
	Afternoon: 5-4-3-2-1 over cross country course, plus SGP
Tuesday	Morning: long loop
	Afternoon: 40- to 50-minute easy run, plus SGP
Wednesday	Morning: short loop
	Afternoon: Lewis and Clark, Gonzaga Prep, and East Valley at Mead (JV race at 4:40 p.m., varsity at 5:40 p.m.)
Thursday	Morning: long loop
	Afternoon: 30 minutes of Oregon drill, plus SGP
Friday	Morning: optional run from home, top-14 runners traveling to Stanford (depart Mead at 7 a.m.)
	Afternoon: light 30-minute run, plus SGP
Saturday	Varsity at Stanford, others run 5-mile (8 km) tempo Prairie Loop
Sunday	Easy 60- to 75-minute run

Notes: The morning run was a staple at Mead and a cornerstone for building a culture of running at the school. It took commitment from everyone on the team to be up and ready to run before school. There were a few loops to choose from, but the long loop generally was a 30-minute run. The short loop was roughly 20 minutes. The morning sessions were just something a little extra to get the legs loose.

> *continued*

> continued

WEEK 6

Monday	Morning: long loop
	Afternoon: power lines (run single file along Waikiki Road at easy pace), plus SGP
Tuesday	Morning: long loop
	Afternoon: 30- to 40-minute run, plus 12 grass strides, plus SGP
Wednesday	Morning: short loop, easy
	Afternoon: bus departs at 12:15 p.m. to GSL meet in Clarkston (frosh/JV race at 4:40 p.m., varsity race at 5:40 p.m., return to Mead at 10 p.m.)
Thursday	Morning: long loop
	Afternoon: 60-minute fun run, Nike BBQ at 5 p.m.
Friday	Morning: short loop
	Afternoon: College Day, easy 30 minutes, plus SGP
Saturday	9 a.m. practice on the track, 35-45 drill (8-12 laps), then easy 20 minutes, then 6 × 300-meter interval cut-downs at 54-52-50-48-46-44 seconds
Sunday	60-80 minutes at conversational pace

Notes: Our power lines loop was an eight-mile (13 km) rectangular loop that included a stretch beneath some power lines. It rolled a bit, and the terrain looked like something from Kenya or Ethiopia. The route came up to a steep hill and then went over toward the college campuses of Whitworth and Gonzaga before heading back to Mead. My note about running single file along Waikiki Road was for safety's sake because the sidewalk we followed was narrow before breaking off at the power lines.

The 60-minute fun run was for the most part unstructured. I wanted the kids to run wherever they wanted, stay moving for an hour, and then return to celebrate. This particular year, Nike was touring around with a van and they stopped at Mead and cooked barbecue for us.

College Day is a term I coined for days when I wanted the guys to have the independence to choose. It was a light day. Sometimes it would be the afternoon before a football game. On College Day, runners did whatever they wanted. There was no meeting, no discussion, no order. The guys were good at figuring out a run they wanted to do. When you train kids to run free, sometimes you have to take your hands off the reins and let them explore that freedom.

The Saturday workout was all about changing gears. This was an amended version of the Oregon 30-40 drill. It is a continuous string of 200 meters, switching from 35-second pace to 45-second pace, back and forth, for 8 to 12 laps. Then, we did 6 × 300-meter intervals where we tried to hit specific times, going faster on each successive interval. There was a 100-meter recovery jog between the 300s. We wanted to get to the point where the guys were hitting closing speed at the end. This was a good workout for polishing up speed.

WEEK 7

Monday	Morning: long loop
	Afternoon: easy 50 minutes, plus SGP
Tuesday	Morning: long loop
	Afternoon: 5-3-1-3 drill (date pace, 2-mile (3.2 km) pace, closing pace, easy), four sets over home cross country course, plus SGP
Wednesday	Morning: long loop
	Afternoon: 40 to 50 minutes easy, varsity goes with Coach Daratha to St. George's, plus SGP
Thursday	Morning: long loop
	Afternoon: 30 minutes of Oregon drill, plus SGP
Friday	Morning: short loop
	Afternoon: bus departs at 1 p.m. for Richland, easy 30 minutes running and studying course, plus work on starts and finishes
Saturday	Richland Invitational, return to Spokane at 7 p.m.
Sunday	Easy 60- to 80-minute run

Notes: The 5-3-1-3 drill was held on the cross country course. I wheeled certain sections of it and put down cones. The workout began with a 500-meter section at date pace, a 300 at slightly faster 3,200-meter pace, a 100 at closing pace and an easy 300 to recover. Then we repeated for a total of four sets.

On Wednesday, assistant Scott Daratha drove the varsity seven over to St. George's, which had some fun trails. It gave the varsity guys a chance to do something different and special together. I stayed back at Mead and oversaw the workout for everyone else.

WEEK 8

Monday	Morning: long loop
	Afternoon: 5-4-3-2-1 fartlek on grass, plus SGP
Tuesday	Morning: long loop
	Afternoon: bus departs at 2:50 for Siemers Farm for light run and work on starts and finishes
Wednesday	Morning: short loop
	Afternoon: out of class at 2:10 p.m., bus departs at 2:25 p.m. for Siemers Farm for GSL meet against Mt. Spokane and West Valley (frosh and JV run at 4:10 p.m., varsity at 5:10 p.m., return to Mead at 6:45 p.m.)
Thursday	Morning: long loop
	Afternoon: 40- to 50-minute run followed by 12 grass strides, plus SGP
Friday	Morning: easy 20 minutes
	Afternoon: photos at 2:45 in blue sweats, light 30-minute run, plus SGP
Saturday	Vans leave at 9 a.m. for Seven Mile course, followed by 3 × mile (1,600 m) at flow pace; cool-down
Sunday	60-70 minutes easy running

Notes: The midweek Greater Spokane League meet was at Siemers Farm, a course that is laid out on an orchard.

On Saturday, we wanted to get over to Seven Mile because we knew we had a big meet coming up against Ferris, our big rivals. We wanted to get over there and learn that course. We broke it into three sections of one mile and ran each piece a little faster than 5K date pace.

> *continued*

> *continued*

WEEK 9

Monday	Morning: long loop
	Afternoon: in groups, run cross country course single file, followed by 3 × 200-meter cut-downs, plus SGP
Tuesday	Morning: long loop, stretch only (no gutbusters or push-ups)
	Afternoon: easy 30-minute run, plus SGP
Wednesday	Morning: short loop
	Afternoon: out of school at 2, bus departs at 2:20 p.m., meet vs. Rogers, Ferris, and North Central at Seven Mile course, return to Mead at 6:45 p.m.
Thursday	Morning: long loop
	Afternoon: top seven go to St. George, everyone else 20-minute run on grass followed by 12 grass strides, plus SGP
Friday	Morning: long loop
	Afternoon: frosh and JV easy jog over course, plus 3 × start and finish, varsity run 40 minutes, plus 12 grass strides
Saturday	Morning: frosh and JV championship, arrive at 9:15 a.m. (frosh boys race at 10:40 a.m., JV boys race at 11:50 a.m.)
	Afternoon: 3 p.m., varsity workout is fartlek
Sunday	Light 60- to 80-minute run

Notes: This week marked the end of the competitive season for the bulk of the team, with the district championships for 9th grade and junior varsity athletes. Many of them turned in their uniforms and completed their season that week. A hearty group of 10 to 12 typically wanted to stay on and continue to hang with the varsity guys and train with them through the state championship meet.

WEEK 10

Monday	Morning: long loop
	Afternoon: 40-minute run plus 12 grass strides
Tuesday	Morning: long loop
	Afternoon: 6 × 800 meters, then cool down
Wednesday	Morning: long loop
	Afternoon: easy 40- to 50-minute run
Thursday	Morning: long loop
	Afternoon: 1 × 500, 400, 300, 200, 100, 100 meters (stride/no time)
Friday	Morning: short loop
	Afternoon: varsity jogs regional course, others run 40 minutes easy
Saturday	Regionals at Deer Park; van departs at 10 a.m., others 5-4-3-2-1 fartlek
Sunday	Easy 60- to 80-minute run

Notes: The Thursday workout on the track was intended to be a sharpener. There was no watch on the intervals, but they should have been done at a nice, crisp pace.

WEEK 11

Monday	Morning: long loop
	Afternoon: 40-minute run plus 12 grass strides
Tuesday	Morning: long loop
	Afternoon: two-man, 300-meter relay
Wednesday	Morning: short loop
	Afternoon: easy run at St. George's
Thursday	Morning: short loop
	Afternoon: Oregon drill, 20 minutes with racing spikes on
Friday	Travel to the Class 4A state championship meet in Pasco, 30-minute run on the course, including three starts and three closes to the finish line
Saturday	State championship race day
Sunday	Easy 60-90 minute run

Notes: Every year we did the same thing the week of the state cross country meet. We rested and prepared and went to the starting line ready to rip.

Because of state rules, I was not allowed to coach the team after the season was completed. The week after state was typically downtime, but I gave workouts to an assistant coach, who kept the top guys going so they could represent themselves and the school at postseason meets such as BorderClash and Nike Cross Nationals Northwest Regional, and if they made it through that, Nike Cross Nationals.

Planning the Season

In the previous section, I detailed workout plans broken down week by week and day by day. To construct your own plan, it's important to first set in place a yearly cycle that creates a purpose and rhythm. That sets the tone for what comes next, layering the season's workout plan on top of the competitive schedule. Your schedule will in some ways determine the pattern of your week, varying from easy days to hard days. For example, our league meets fell on Wednesdays, so our training plans reflected that. We didn't go hard on Tuesday with a meet the next day.

Once the schedule is in place, you can use the principles shared in chapter 4 (and the previous season plan) to guide your training plan. Because our week usually had a Wednesday and Saturday set aside for races, the rest of our week looked like this:

GENERIC WORKOUT WEEK

Monday	**Medium day**
	Morning: light run 2-5 miles (3.2-8 km)
	Afternoon: run 5-8 miles (8-13 km), plus 12 ×100 meters grass strides; plus SGP
Tuesday	**Easy day**
	Morning: light run 3-5 miles (4.8-8 km)
	Afternoon: review course, plus three or four starts and three or four finishes, making sure racing shoes are appropriate for conditions, plus SGP or weights
Wednesday	**Race day**
	If it was an "easy" competition, we might call this tempo day.
Thursday	**Oregon drill day or fartlek day**
	Morning: light run 2-5 miles (3.2-8 km)
	Afternoon: some variation of shorter interval workout at tune-up pace plus grass strides or hills, plus SGP or weights
Friday	**Easy day**
	Morning: light run 2-4 miles (3.2-6.4 km)
	Afternoon: recovery run 3-6 miles (4.8-9.6 km) plus SGP
Saturday	**Invitational race day or quality-workout day**
	If you do not have a race, then do a great quality workout: 3 × 1-mile runs at date pace with 5 minutes of easy jogging for recovery, 20 minutes of easy running, and finish with 6 × 300-meter cutdowns, starting at race pace and cutting each by 2 seconds.
Sunday	**On your own**
	Ideally, a long easy run of 60 to 90 minutes

Keeping a Journal

All the great runners keep a journal or log of the workouts and mileage that they do. I used to keep one when I was coming up as a runner, and they are too important to ignore. I never made it mandatory, but it was a given that if you were going to be one of the varsity guys, go on the road trips, get the cool black T-shirt at the end of the season, and be serious about winter and summer training, that a journal was part of the deal.

For decades that meant using a trusty spiral notebook and writing everything down with a pen or pencil. Nowadays, some kids do it online. Figure 5.1 recreates a section of my journal in the week leading up to the NCAA cross country championship during my junior year in college. I placed 31st and Oregon won the team title.

There are many reasons for keeping a journal. First, it's a place for runners to chart their mileage for the week so that they can see progression from year to year. It's important to be able to make comparisons and know the differences in quality and volume from one year to the next. It's a good way to chart where a runner is headed.

Secondly, a journal is a place where runners can record how they feel. I like runners to keep track of the temperature, make note of what the weather is like, and also record their resting heart rate in the morning and their weight. Some of this data may be more or less important to you, but there is value in having a permanent record and a guideline of where your athletes are currently.

If resting heart rate, for instance, is elevated some morning, it will tell you that something isn't quite right. Perhaps your runner is coming down with an illness. Maybe it's a sign of overtraining or something else. When you

Figure 5.1 Sample Page From Tyson's 1971 Journal

Wednesday, Nov. 17
Morning: 6 miles (9.6 km) easy
Afternoon: 7-8 miles (11-13 km) with Pre and the gang up 29th to Jefferson and back down 13th. Ran mile around the track, too. 4 × 110 yards

Thursday, Nov. 18
Morning: 6 miles
Afternoon: 1-mile warm-up. 2 × 220 yards (27.5, 27.5). Went on 5-mile (8 km) run through valley. Finished with 4 × 110

Friday, Nov. 19
Morning: 6 miles
Afternoon: 8 × 330 yards (47-48 sec.), 110 jog between each. Light 3-mile (4.8 km) run around Fairmount Avenue.

Saturday, Nov. 20
Morning: 4 (6.4 km) miles easy. Flew to Knoxville, Tennessee, for NCAA x-country championships. 3 miles light at 9:00 p.m. in Knoxville.

Sunday, Nov. 21
Chilly. Ran 3-4 miles over the Fox Den golf course x-country course. Rather hilly, really a tough course. Cold, windy, cloudy.

Monday, Nov. 22
NCAA x-country championships in Knoxville, Tennessee. Clear, cold, windy morning. 35 degrees (1.7 C) at 11:00 a.m. 312 runners. I started rather quickly—4:36. At that point, I was around 150th place. I then moved up the second steep hill and moved into position. I came in contact with Dave Harper of WSU and went with him for the next two miles or more and was about 50th after three miles. This actually felt pretty good. I was about 15:07. Then I started up the second steep hill again where I caught Marty Liquori of Villanova. I stayed with him all the rest of the way. It was tough that last mile. I ended up 31st in 30:34. Just three seconds from being All-American, but we won the team title. Greatest experience of my life.

see changes written on the pages of a journal, you are more apt to consider them and their meanings.

A well-detailed journal can also come in handy if runners fall into a rut. In those times, you can go back and see what they were doing in their training when they felt great and begin to understand what workouts they respond to best and which ones leave them drained. What caused the rut? A lack of sleep? A fluctuation in weight? Illness? Journals help runners remember what works well and serve as a reminder to get back on an even keel.

As a coach, I do not keep a journal. I do, however, save all of the workouts. Over time a coach becomes dialed into what works and what doesn't. I never felt I needed to write down what works and what doesn't. Keeping the workouts gives coaches a feeling for that.

From year to year you might find it necessary to make adjustments. If you have a veteran team with lots of high-quality runners, you might want to devise a schedule that bumps up the intensity or the mileage a bit. If your program is going through a building phase and the roster is dominated by freshmen and sophomores, you could dial back the workload and add fun activities to make sure that your young runners stay engaged.

In my experience, there was not a significant shift one way or the other from year to year. When you have a healthy program of 50 to 100 runners, the numbers generally work out so that training groups remain fairly consistent.

Guiding Principles

Writing workouts is an important aspect of coaching because there are a lot of moving parts. It's not always easy to come up with a one-size-fits-all plan that's good for everybody. When I write workouts, they are all derived from the five principles of the Oregon system discussed earlier in this chapter. It's important to remain flexible and be able to adapt to changing situations. Primarily, this relates to keeping workloads safe when athletes are fatigued and managing the diverse needs of athletes that come up, including injuries.

- **Don't mindlessly repeat what you've done.** When I started at Mead, I conducted a one-hour workout on the track at the start of the cross country season. And in those early days, everyone went the full hour. But as I went on, I got a little smarter about it and asked the rookies to run for half an hour. A full hour was too much. The thinking you apply to workouts adapts and evolves over time.

- **Be proactive regarding injuries.** I was fairly lucky at Mead with regard to injuries. It was always one of my goals to have healthy athletes. However, one of the best athletes I had in my final years at the school was Laef Barnes, who didn't run at the state track meet as a junior or senior because of stress fractures. He was probably the best guy in Washington both years in the mile (1,600 m) and I felt bad for him. Maybe one day a week off for certain kids, where they cross-train instead of run, is better.

- **One size doesn't fit all.** It's not easy to manage each runner on the team. The decisions you make to help one athlete through an injury may not work for somebody else.

- **Establish trust regarding injuries.** Communication with athletes is the key to avoiding overuse injuries, but getting them to talk to you and be honest about what's going on and how they're feeling is not easy. The last thing a high school athlete wants is to sound like a whiner. But that's precisely the situation that brings on trouble.

- **Individualize workouts as necessary.** Some kids should have an extra day of easy workouts. Tweaking workouts for each person is not a bad thing. Yes, it is easier to cluster the runners, but you have to do what's right for the health of the team. You can break athletes into groups based on date pace. Each group performs the same workout, but their target times are adjusted. This way the groups with faster date paces are challenged, and the groups with slower date paces can focus on improving and not just trying to keep up.

- **Put runners into groups.** I generally separated my guys into groups. The A group was the varsity top seven. The B group was the next seven. The C group was big and consisted of hard-working kids. And there was usually a D group and an E group for slower and younger kids. Those C, D, and E groups had about 10 kids apiece, and I appointed a leader for each "posse." Each group took on elements of the same workout plan but at varying degrees of intensity. Ultimately, you want kids to complete workouts thinking, "I conquered it."

Maintaining Proper Nutrition

A lot of information is available on proper nutrition, choosing foods that are healthy, and maintaining a balanced diet. I don't want to complicate the game. To me, a proper diet is all about moderation. I told my teams to indulge in fresh vegetables and fresh fruit rather than a bunch of junk food. When eating a healthy diet, they would be sick less often and would be able to power their engine more efficiently. I never had a rule against drinking soda, but I certainly didn't recommend it. Over time, we evolved into a team that didn't drink soda. That is generally the case across the country.

A regular breakfast is a good thing. We had bananas and cereal available in the locker room in the mornings. Once a week during the fall season at Mead, the guys went to a parents' house after their morning run for a hot breakfast of pancakes or waffles. For lunch, I recommend keeping it simple, especially on meet days. Peanut butter and jelly

sandwiches are a good thing. Carrot sticks or healthy snacks are preferred over French fries and pizza. You want good fuel that's easy to digest.

Now, you may be wondering about our Monday pizza nights. Yes, we did that. There was also a salad bar, and the kids usually chose water over pop. They made those choices for themselves because they understood the value of eating right. Unhealthy choices such as candy just aren't worth it. When your team eats healthy foods, they remain calm and focused. That's what we preached. But I also think it's OK to celebrate on occasion with ice cream.

Some items that are healthy have a track record of not working well. Apples and oranges contain an acid can cause side aches. I'm not sure if there's science behind that observation or not, but anecdotally, I've seen evidence to back that up. Also, I'd stay away from milk at lunchtime. I have found that on race day it's best to stop eating three and a half to four hours before a race.

Getting Enough Sleep

Distance runners require a minimum of eight solid hours of sleep in a perfect world. In bed by 10:00 p.m. and then up and ready to run at 6:00 a.m. Serious runners quickly understand that these hours are sacred and that sleep is necessary. Why would you go to bed late on the weekend and upset your rhythm? The daily workout load is laborious, and it simply doesn't work unless there is respect for the value of sleep. If you're not committed to doing everything associated with training and racing the right way, then why do it at all?

It takes a little time for high school runners to get into a consistent daily pattern, but life as a runner means adhering to a schedule. Consistency in sleep, eating, training, homework, and family time is part of the daily balance that is necessary for success.

I was a worrywart as a high school kid. I tossed and turned in bed at night and was insecure about whether I'd done everything necessary to be ready for a race. I've learned since then that you have to train yourself to fall asleep. You learn to block out distractions or unproductive thoughts and worries and just drift off. One rule of thumb is to avoid any caffeinated drinks in the evening. Another suggestion is to listen to light music. Pre taught me to not think after my head hit the pillow. It's not easy and it takes some effort to shut off an active brain, but try to get your athletes to block out the stresses of the day.

Some say the most important night's sleep isn't the one right before a big race, but two nights before. I fall back on consistency as the name of the game. As a coach, try to alleviate concerns or worries so that your runners are relaxed enough to get the sleep they need. The good athletes in your program will quickly learn and understand how important sleep is. Any time you are up at 6:00 a.m., you're going to be tired by 9:00 p.m. You run, go to class all day, work out, and then eat. By the end of that, you're dead meat.

Summary

Planning for the season begins with a bedrock belief that running is a year-round sport and a lifestyle. That isn't an easy hill to climb, but if you can make some headway, you can begin to apply the principles of training, map out a schedule that makes sense, and help your athletes understand the details that go into building a better runner.

- Cross country is a year-round sport, and there are no days off in the process of becoming a better runner. It's a lifestyle.

- The five principles I learned at Oregon—moderation, progression, variation, adaptation, and callousing—are tried and true and inform every aspect of my training plans.

- Time trials can help establish an early-season pecking order, but they are also valuable as rehearsals for competition.

- The competition schedule establishes how to create flow and structure in each week's workout plans.

- Encourage your runners to keep a journal to record their mileage, their feelings, the weather, their heart rates, and anything else that might be helpful to refer to later.

- Pay attention to proper nutrition and encourage athletes to get the sleep and rest they need.

CHAPTER 6

Preparing for Practices

This chapter reviews a typical day at practice. It describes the stretching, gut-busters, and push-ups (SGP) routine, explains the goals of each practice, shows how to conduct a team meeting, gives tips for conducting a workout, and explains what to do and say to close a practice. Further, it explains how a first practice differs from a postseason practice. Each runner should understand how to make each day on the calendar meaningful and count for something important.

Mental Preparation: Daily Practice

Runners must mentally prepare themselves for practice. The best runners are not always the ones in top shape. Mental attitude separates the champions from the athletes. Your runners should practice these guidelines for daily workouts.

- Mentally set aside physical limitations that might hamper the workout.
- Mentally set aside schoolwork that might occupy your thinking.

- Enjoy each practice session no matter the pace, the course, the weather, or the distance.
- Set mental goals to measure daily practices. Understand in advance what benchmarks need to be met to fulfill the requirements of the session.
- Support each other! (As 1972 Olympic 800-meter champion Dave Wottle said of his Bowling Green University team, "We all train in a group and we all draw strength from the group.")

Each day's training is mapped out with the goal of producing improvement. Your runners should expect regular progress to occur. Help your runners mentally prepare themselves to excel in their training by telling them what to expect and how each piece fits into the big picture. Use your energy to get them excited and ready to attack the day's work.

Mornings

Over my 20 years at Mead, we were out the door for our morning run at 6:30. One time in all of those years I was about two minutes late and the guys razzed me to death about it. Ninety-nine percent of the time I arrived at the school at 6:00 a.m., and most of the runners on the team arrived about 6:25. This was our ritual, a light 20- to 30-minute run every morning.

The morning run teaches kids something important and gets them to adopt a healthy habit. Morning is a beautiful time to think, to process, and to be creative. It also connects the kids and reinforces the feeling that their commitment is shared. They'll also feel better during class. Not all kids embrace the early wake-up call and run right away. Maybe it takes three weeks or four, but once they get in the habit and adjust the time they go to bed, they grow to love the pattern.

The morning run is a fixture and something that begins on the first day of school and lasts throughout the school year. In Spokane, it sometimes got bitterly cold in the winter, so we occasionally had to make adjustments for the weather. Lots of times we went out and did our run anyway, with lots of layers. After all, we figured, we're "Spokane People." But if there was black ice or it was especially cold, we changed the venue and ran through the halls of the school. If it was just snow, then we went outside, loving it. The powder landing on our stocking caps and on our cheeks and noses, and the cold, crisp air in our lungs—it was invigorating. There's nothing like running through the snow when the Christmas lights are on. We slowed down a little and were more cautious, but as Don Kardong (1976 Olympic marathoner and author) said, "No runner ever got hurt because he was forced to slow down."

Today, it seems like more kids have access to fitness gyms with treadmills, stationary bikes, ellipticals, stair climbers, and other cardio machines. When the weather forces you inside, you find a way to adapt without losing your daily rhythm.

Stretches, Gut-Busters, and Push-Ups (SGP)

Running takes up the bulk of each day's workout, and there is no substitute for what variety—long and slow, short and fast, fartlek, tempo, hills—does to build cardiorespiratory fitness and leg strength. But flexibility is important. Core strength is essential to any athletic pursuit. And push-ups are a simple, easy way to address upper-body and arm strength. These activities are essential to injury prevention. The formula for implementing these facets of training varies from place to place, and it evolved over time at Mead.

SGP was a staple of our practice days, Monday through Friday. All of these pieces fit together nicely at the end of the workout. We did these stretches and exercises as we were cooling down and sometimes a little bit tired, too.

Stretches

We almost always did these on the grass and often did them barefoot. The positions of these stretches borrow heavily from yoga. This routine is intended to flow from one stretch to the next. The routine takes about 20 minutes and should be done in order so one position transitions smoothly into the next.

KNEE RISE

Kneeling, place hands on hips. Sit back on heels and hold (see figure 6.1*a*). Rise up to knees again, with thighs and abdomen perpendicular to ground and shoulders square (see figure 6.1*b*). This stretch loosens the thighs, ankles, and shins. Do 5 to 10 repetitions.

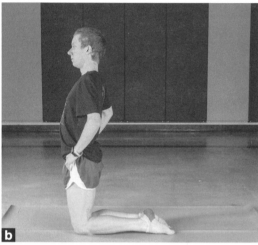

Figure 6.1 Knee rise.

DOWNWARD REACH

With feet flat on the ground (see figure 6.2*a*), bend at the waist with torso leaning forward and hands on the ground (see figure 6.2*b*). Keep legs and back straight. Hold for 45 to 60 seconds. Repeat several times.

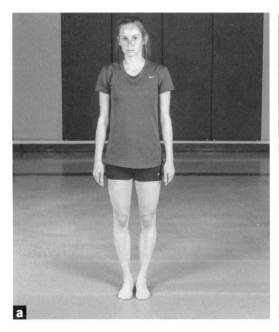

Figure 6.2 Downward reach.

TORSO PRESS

With pelvis on the ground and legs extended backward (see figure 6.3), press torso up with arms straight, creating a line from the top of the head to the hands. Hold for 45 to 60 seconds. Repeat a couple of times.

Figure 6.3   Torso press.

HIP STRETCH

With one leg extended straight back, bring the forward leg to a 90-degree angle with chest positioned over the top. Place hands flat on the ground on either side of the foot and shift weight forward (see figure 6.4a). This stretches the glutes, groin, and hamstrings. Switch legs so the opposite leg is forward and repeat the stretch. Repeat the stretch while extending one arm under the knee to grab the opposite arm, like a brace (see figure 6.4b). This will deepen the stretch.

Figure 6.4   Hip stretch.

SUPPORTED PIGEON POSE

Come down to the ground, with one leg extended back and the forward leg bent at the knee with the shin on the ground and hands on either side of the knee. Keep shoulders square, back leg as straight as possible. The foot of the forward leg can be tucked into the groin area (see figure 6.5a). This stretch is good for the iliotibial (IT) band. Hold for 60 to 90 seconds, then switch legs so the opposite is forward and repeat. Do a few slow, relaxed push-ups in this position, with chest out over the knee and repeat with the other leg forward (see figure 6.5b). Finally, stretch forward over the bent leg and reach the chest forward and low over the thigh. Stretch forward and reach with the hands (see figure 6.5c). Repeat the whole exercise with the other leg forward.

Figure 6.5 Supported pigeon pose.

SEATED TRUNK TWIST

From a seated position, bring one leg over the other, with the knee bent next to the chest (see figure 6.6). Push gently on the outside of the knee with the opposite elbow, creating a little bit of torque. This stretches the glutes and the back muscles.

Figure 6.6 Seated trunk twist.

BUTTERFLY STRETCH

Begin seated with the knees out to the sides (see figure 6.7a). Grab the feet with the hands and pull them in close. Press the knees slightly down (see figure 6.7b).

Figure 6.7 Butterfly stretch.

SEATED FORWARD STRETCH

With legs straight out and spread wide, lean forward and try to grab the toes (see figure 6.8). If you can't stretch that far, reach as far down the shins toward the ankle as possible.

Figure 6.8 Seated forward stretch.

SUPINE KNEE PULL

Lie on the ground in a supine position and rest one straight leg forward (see figure 6.9a). Bend the other leg at the knee and pull it toward the chest with both hands. Keep your body as straight as possible (see figure 6.9b). Switch legs and repeat.

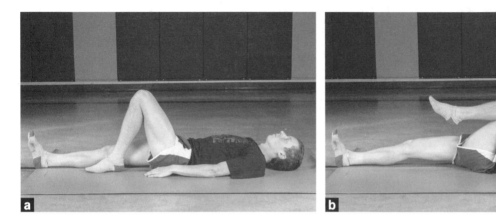

Figure 6.9 Supine knee pull.

SUPINE HAMSTRING STRETCH

Lie on the ground in a supine position, with hands behind the hamstring. Extend the leg so that it is perpendicular to the ground (see figure 6.10a). Bend at the knee and raise the foot several times (see figure 6.10b). Switch legs and repeat.

Figure 6.10 Supine hamstring stretch.

SUPINE LEG STRETCH

Lie on the ground in a supine position (see figure 6.11*a*). Raise the leg and grab the toes with the hand, working to keep the leg as straight as possible (see figure 6.11*b*). Hold the stretch for up to 60 seconds. Switch legs and repeat.

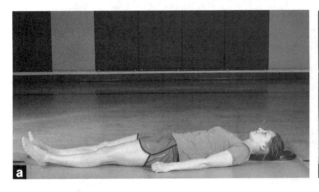 

Figure 6.11 Supine leg stretch.

BACK ROLL

From a seated position, reach forward and touch the toes and then roll backward onto the back and bring the legs overhead (see figure 6.12). Repeat slowly and steadily 5 to 10 times.

Figure 6.12 Back roll.

Gut-Busters

Strong abdominal muscles promote better posture and running mechanics. This routine for developing abdominal and core strength has been adapted over the years at Mead. Some exercises are traditional and others are optional. The team captains generally lead the exercises and set the pace. If younger athletes can't complete all of the reps, it's OK. Keep moving from one exercise to the next, like a circuit, in the following order.

FLICKERS

Lie on the back with fingers laced behind the head (see figure 6.13a). With legs out straight, flutter them up and down, keeping the legs as straight as possible (see figure 6.13b). Perform 30 reps.

Figure 6.13   Flickers.

LEGS OVERHEAD

From the same position on the back as for flickers, rock back onto the shoulder blades so that the legs aim all the way over the head, roughly parallel to the ground (see figure 6.14a). Then roll forward so that the legs extend out in front but do not touch the ground, and the back comes off the ground and remains straight (see figure 6.14b). Perform 30 reps.

Figure 6.14   Legs overhead.

KNEES TO CHEST

Begin with the back flat on the ground and legs straight. Bring knees to chest (see figure 6.15a) and then shoot the legs out, with toes pointed forward (see figure 6.15b). Again, feet don't touch the ground. Perform 30 reps.

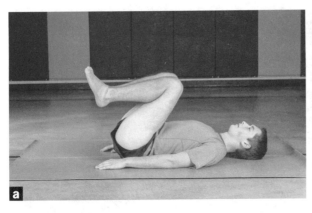

Figure 6.15   Knees to chest.

CRUNCHER

Lying on the back with knees over chest (see figure 6.16a), pull the head forward and use the abdominal muscles to hold each rep for a moment (see figure 6.16b). Perform 50 reps.

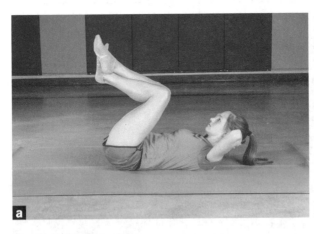

Figure 6.16   Cruncher.

CRISSCROSS

Lying on the ground, raise legs into the air toward the sky and brace the waist over the ground (see figure 6.17a), cross legs back and forth from side to side (see figure 6.17b). Perform 10 reps.

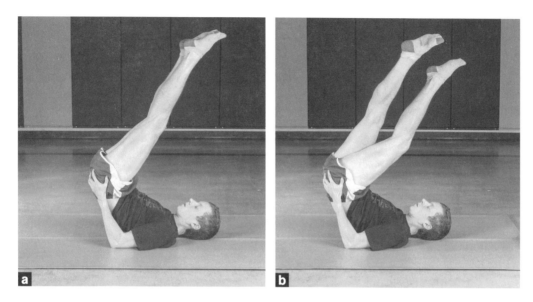

Figure 6.17   Crisscross.

BICYCLE

From the same position as the crisscross (see figure 6.18a), rotate legs as if on a bicycle, easy and slowly (see figure 6.18b). Perform 10 reps.

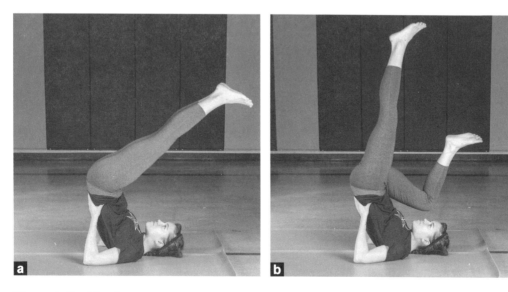

Figure 6.18   Bicycle.

HIP ROTATION

With the back flat on the ground, bend legs at the knees and slowly rock them from side to side about 160 degrees (see figure 6.19). Knees don't touch the ground. Perform 10 reps.

Figure 6.19   Hip rotation.

LEG LIFTER

Lie flat on the back (see figure 6.20*a*). Keeping the knees locked and legs straight and using the abdominal muscles to do the work, raise the heels about 20 inches (50 cm) off the ground for about one second (see figure 6.20*b*). Hands can be behind the head or along the sides on the ground. Perform 50 reps without letting the heels touch the ground.

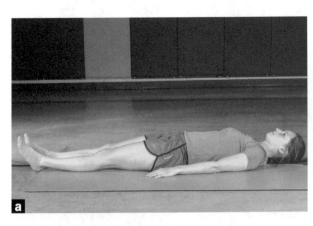

Figure 6.20   Leg lifter.

SWITCHER

Start on the back with bent knees (see figure 6.21a). With fingers laced behind head, like a cruncher, bring the head forward to the outside of one knee and then the other (see figure 6.21b). The rotational element works additional abdominal muscles. Perform 40 reps.

Figure 6.21 Switcher.

ARCH THE BACK

From the same position as the switcher with knees still up and hands behind the head (see figure 6.22a), pull forward and lunge the chest forward (see figure 6.22b) before rocking back down to the back and returning to the start position. This is a quick, dynamic movement. It may be avoided if an athlete has a back injury. This is a tough exercise and requires strength. The feet stay off the ground. Perform 30 reps.

Figure 6.22 Arch the back.

Optional Gut-Busters

Optional abdominal exercises come next. Usually the captain or leader of the exercises will pick one stretch from a variety of options and do about 50 reps. The optional exercise may follow the previous routine or substitute for one of the previous gut-buster exercises.

SQUIGGLIES

From a reclined position, with butt on the ground and knees bent, fold arms across the chest (see figure 6.23a) and twist the torso in one direction and then the other. Do the first 20 with legs bent (see figure 6.23b) and the final 10 with legs straight out in front, heels off the ground 6 to 12 inches (15-30 cm) (see figure 6.23c).

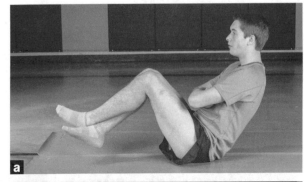

Figure 6.23 Squigglies.

ON YOUR SIDE

This is a modified cruncher. Begin by lying on one hip with feet resting on the ground (see figure 6.24a). With hands behind the head for support, raise the torso to target specific abdominal muscles (see figure 6.24b). Perform 30 reps on each side.

Figure 6.24 On your side.

ROBBIE-O

We named this after one of our alums, Rob Aubrey. It combines elements of squigglies and bicycle (see figure 6.25a). The pedal motion happens in front rather than overhead, with the torso twisting back and forth (see figure 6.25b). Perform 50 reps.

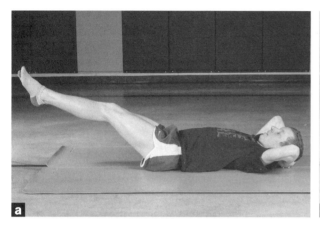

Figure 6.25 Robbie-O.

DIETER BAUMANN

This is an homage to the 1992 Olympic 5,000-meter champion from Germany. The starting position is like a push-up, with legs straight back, body facing the ground. Support weight on the forearms positioned directly below the shoulders and head (see figure 6.26). Get into position and hold it, back straight, for 60 seconds or so. This exercise also lends itself well to a team contest: Who can hold it the longest?

Figure 6.26 Dieter Baumann.

Fifty Push-Ups

Conclude your SGP session with push-ups, which are a simple but effective exercise to address upper-body strength (see figure 6.27). Start with 20 push-ups at a nice steady pace. Then pause 5 to 30 seconds. The length of our pause depended on who led the exercise.

Do 15 more at a slightly slower pace and pause again. And then do 10 in slow motion and pause once more. Finish with 5 push-ups at an even slower rate, holding the position longer at the top and bottom of each rep, con-

centrating on correct posture and the work of each muscle involved.

Once every couple of weeks, we made a contest out of the push-ups. We split the group in half, maybe 25 guys on each side. And each side did something like a relay, with each member of the team doing 50 quality push-ups, followed by the next person, and then the next. Near the end of this competition, the team was cheering for the final members of the team to complete their push-ups in order to "win" the day.

Weight Lifting

During the cross country season, I did not emphasize weight training because there was limited access to Mead's weight room during the afternoons. Plus, with attention paid to stretching, gut-busters, and push-ups I didn't think weight lifting during the season was necessary.

However, I did occasionally take smaller groups of highly committed varsity guys into the weight room before the season or in the off-season. I put together a 20-minute routine of 10 stations that we did two or three days a week: Monday and Friday and sometimes Wednesday. Athletes should flow from one station to the next without waiting, which is why it's ideal to do it with a smaller group.

The purpose of weight training for cross country is not to build muscle so much as to address weaknesses, particularly in the upper body, and to become a better overall athlete. I suggest applying weight training lightly to the year-round cycle, if at all. Feel free to mix up the order of the following exercises.

FIGURE 6.27 Push-up.

DIP

This is a good warm-up exercise. Use parallel dip bars and begin with arms straight and then lower the body until arms are bent to a 90-degree angle (see figure 6.28a). Then push back up to the starting position (see figure 6.28b). Perform three sets of 10 reps.

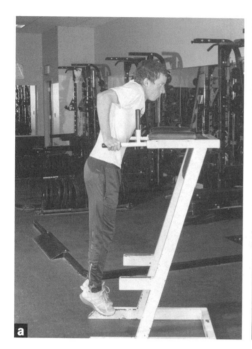

Figure 6.28   Dip.

BENCH

Rookies might start off with 40 pounds (18 kg); veterans might do as much as 100 pounds (45 kg). The key is being able to do 10 reps and not a max effort. Begin with the weight a couple of inches (about 5 cm) over the chest (see figure 6.29a) and push it up, controlling the weight (see figure 6.29b). Perform three sets of 10 reps.

Figure 6.29   Bench.

FRENCH CURL WITH DUMBBELL

Perform behind-the-head curls with 5 to 10 pounds (2.3-4.5 kg) to work the triceps. Hold the weights slightly behind the shoulder (see figure 6.30a) and straighten the arm upward to complete each rep (see figure 6.30b). Perform three sets of 10 reps.

Figure 6.30 French curl with dumbbell.

ABDOMINAL BOARD

Lying on a slant bench, reach back over the head and grab the edge of the bench or padding (see figure 6.31a) and use the abdominal muscles to lift the feet over the head (see figure 6.31b). Keep the legs straight. This exercise allows time for the arms and legs to recover from the other exercises. Return to this exercise after completing two or three of the other circuit stations. Perform three sets of 10 reps each time.

Figure 6.31 Abdominal board.

HAMSTRING CURL

Lying facedown, position heels under the weight (see figure 6.32a). Raise the weight by bending knees and contracting the hamstring muscles (see figure 6.32b). Keep the weight light, just 20 to 50 pounds (9-23 kg). Progress by performing each rep more slowly rather than by adding weight. Perform three sets of 10 reps.

Figure 6.32 Hamstring curl.

BOX STEP-UP

Holding a lightweight barbell, 15 to 40 pounds (6.8-18kg) (see figure 6.33a), step up onto a 24-inch (60 cm) box with one foot (see figure 6.33b) and rise up on the toes (see figure 6.33c). Alternate right and left. Do three sets of 10 reps.

Figure 6.33 Box step-up.

LIGHT ROUTINE DUMBBELL

With a 5- to 10-pound (2.3-4.5 kg) dumbbell in each hand, run in place in front a mirror and pay attention to form. The weight moves from shoulder to hip with good arm action (see figure 6.34). Perform three sets of 10 reps.

Figure 6.34   Light routine dumbbell.

MILITARY PRESS

Use a light weight, 30 to 50 pounds (14-23 kg), and focus on form. Begin with the weight at shoulder height under the chin (see figure 6.35a). Press upward until arms are straight (see figure 6.35b). Remain in control of the bar. The goal is not body building but simply enhancing upper-body strength and working on tone. Perform three sets of 10 reps.

Figure 6.35   Military press.

Warm-Up and Cool-Down Routines

The warm-up for a workout and a race is the same and it's simple. I suggest a 15-minute jog followed by a restroom break and then light stretching. For a race or an interval workout, the athlete puts on spikes and double-knots the laces. Next the athlete runs two or three laps, striding the straightaways and jogging the curves. That's it.

Maintain consistency in your warm-up by doing it the same way every time. It promotes a sense of rhythm that leads into the workout. Think of it as a diagnostic exercise in which each athlete is communicating with their bodies and receiving feedback that all muscle groups are fit and ready to go. The warm-up is also a good time to transition mentally and psychologically from the classroom. A smooth transition period promotes a feeling of confidence throughout the workout.

The cool down at the end of a workout should be a light recovery run of 10-30 minutes. If more time allows, you could also do some grass strides or soft-surface intervals. If you have foam rollers, use them for a self-massage of the legs. Some athletes also like to use an ice bath to literally cool down hot, tired legs.

Goals of Practice

Practice is the daily team gathering in which we put the five principles—moderation, progression, variation, adaptation, callousing—into play. Workouts are written in a specific pattern in order to develop mastery of all of the aspects of racing. Some workouts are designed to improve the aerobic engine. Others are meant to teach how to run fast and hold a nonaerobic pace. And still other runs are meant to help the body recover.

You might have noticed in chapter 5, where I outlined how to map out a typical week, that there are never hard days back to back. You want to figure out a pattern of hard-moderate-easy that makes sense when you wrap those workouts around the meet dates on the schedule. Each day, the goal of the athlete is to complete the workout as written by the coach. Some of them are hard and some of them are easy. But each is a brushstroke on the bigger picture, which is revealed over the three months of the cross country season.

Putting Away the Watch

I vividly remember conducting a workout early in my career, an interval session on the track, and coming away convinced that I'd screwed it up. I asked my runners to hit particular times on a blustery day. I didn't adjust the numbers on the workout plan, and the athletes had a difficult time hitting the workout. That made them frustrated.

Sometimes, you have to throw the watch away and worry instead about the effort. You have to be flexible and get back to basics. You have to run like a Kenyan on the high plains of Africa's Rift Valley: free, loose, and unbound by the tools of time and distance. If a high school kid in Eldoret, Kenya, runs the five miles (8 km) from his home to school, he doesn't measure it or time it, he just does it! Treat it like you're in a Jack London short story: man vs. nature. You want your kids above all to put in the effort. They should go home feeling like they conquered their workout.

I spent a lot of time monitoring things like the weather conditions. I wanted to be prepared for what we would face each afternoon. And I learned that if it was windy, there was no sense in holding a stopwatch. It wasn't going to do anybody any good.

Over the years, I came by another nugget of wisdom that related to practice: Never do a hard workout on a Monday. It just doesn't go well. Maybe it's because kids stay up a little bit too late on the weekends, or perhaps they are mentally gearing up for the new week and don't want to start out with a difficult workout. I'm not sure I can explain why, but it's just a bad idea.

Games

Sometimes you need a change of pace in order to get out of a rut and feel alive again. Games can break up the monotony that kids sometimes experience when they've stuck to the plan a little too long and its starts to feel like a grind.

One fall there were forest fires nearby and the air was full of dust and smoke. School administrators came to me and said it wasn't safe to do our workouts outside. So we went into the gym and made the best of it. I came up with something called the Picnic Relays, and the group split into teams for all kinds of shuttle relays: running backward, wheelbarrow races, crab crawls, push-ups, and so on. There is no end to the races you can invent for kids to do in a gym. I ended the Picnic Relays by making all of the guys put their shoes in a pile on the far side of the gym. The final race was for each group to send one runner at a time to the pile, find his shoes, put them on and tie them, and run back. It was a good one to end on.

Games don't normally go on the weekly workout schedule. They are an audible, called by the coach, on a day when the team needs a change-up. Sometimes, when the routine has been formal and by the book for a few weeks, the kids get a little worn out. Some of my favorite games follow.

FOX AND HOUND

1. One person, usually an assistant coach, is the fox and goes out onto the campus with a bag of fun groceries—chips, red licorice, chocolate milk, and so on—and hides with it.

2. The fox may leave a few hints (we used a little bit of white flour) and doesn't have to stay in one spot. But he or she should remain well-hidden because this game has a time limit of one hour.

3. Send out kids (hounds) at intervals, maybe every 10 seconds or so. I went in reverse order of cross country PRs, so the slowest kids went first.

4. When the hounds catch the fox, the game is over. The hound that finds the fox wins the bag of goodies.

At Mead we were fortunate to have a lot of trees. This game might be difficult to play if there is a lack of good hiding spots.

SCAVENGER HUNT

Create a list of objects that you know are somewhat easy to find on your school grounds: a pine cone, a wildflower. Each runner takes the list outside and tries to gather the items. If fall leaves are on the ground, you can ask for the biggest leaf or a yellow leaf, an orange leaf, and a red leaf. List whatever you can think of that makes sense where you are. Create an incentive by offering a prize.

Over spring break for track we held an Easter egg hunt around campus. You can also plant items for your runners to find: bobby pins, pennies, bags of candy. You can create all sorts of competitions around this theme. The point is to keep your team playing, having fun, running, and building team camaraderie.

HIDDEN COLORS

1. Form a large circle with 6 to 10 cones spaced equally from one another and 50 meters from the center. Under each cone is a felt pen, a different color under each cone (see figure 6.36).
2. Create teams of 5 to 10 athletes and station them at home bases about 200 meters away from the circle.
3. The coach stands in the middle with cards that correspond to the color of each felt pen.
4. When the game begins, one runner from each team sprints to the center of the circle and gets a color from the coach and then returns to his or her team. Then the entire team runs together from one cone to the next to find that color.
5. When the team finds the right pen, each member marks a dot on the arm. After replacing the pen back beneath the cone, the team returns to home base.
6. Repeat the process until one team wins.

The game ends when one team has found every marker and has a dot of every color. (The ink should be washable). I asked each team to take the name of a former Mead legend (e.g., Team Chris Lewis or Matt Davis) or another running hero (Team Pre, Team Billy Mills, or Team Ritz.). The winning team got Popsicles (or if it was a hot day, the winners got two and everyone else got one). This game should equate to 10 × 200-meter strides at a minimum, and it also promotes team spirit.

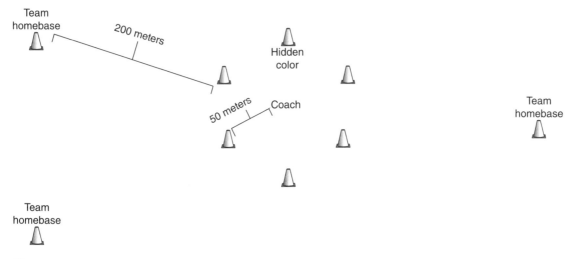

Figure 6.36   Hidden colors setup.

TWO-MAN RELAY

I usually set this up with a 300-meter loop. One runner goes 300 meters and passes the baton to the second runner, who does the same. We make it a 10 × 300-meter race, with each kid running five laps and then jogging in place to recover while the partner is running. It's simple, contains a competitive aspect, and it's fast. We might do this 10 × 300 meters twice so that each runner completes 3,000 meters of hard running.

WATER CUP RELAY

The coach determines how long the relay lasts, usually 20 to 30 minutes.

1. Arrange six cones about 100 meters apart to form a large loop about 600 meters around. Place a 10-gallon (38 L) container of water to designate the start of the loop. Each team needs an empty 1-gallon (3.8 L) container, also near the start-finish point (see figure 6.37).

2. Divide the group into teams of six members and station one member at each cone. The goal is to move the water around the circuit and dump it into the receptacle with as little spillage as possible.

3. Each member of the team has an empty cup. The first runner scoops water from the large container and then runs 100 meters to the first teammate and pours the water into the teammate's cup. The relay continues all the way around the loop.

4. The sixth runner dumps the water into the empty container and then scoops up a fresh cupful and the team runs in the reverse direction.

5. This is a continuous relay. You can go for 20 to 30 minutes. The team that pours the most water into its container is the winner.

The prize for this game could be letting the winning team dump its water over the coach's head.

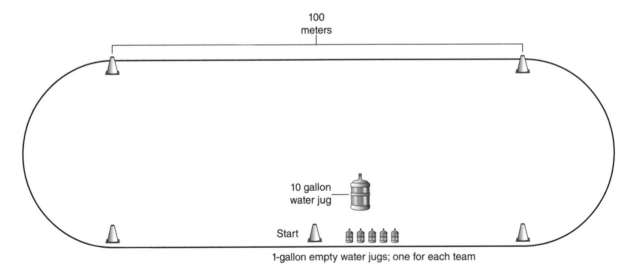

Figure 6.37   Water cup relay setup.

CARD GAME

Create a workout made up of five stages. For example, the workout could progress: 5 × a steep 80-meter hill, 10 minutes of a medium paced run, 5 × a less steep 100-meter hill, 10 minutes of a medium paced run, and 5 × a gradual 200-meter hill. As each athlete completes a stage, deal him or her one card from a deck. At the end of the five stages, everyone has a hand of five cards. Judge the winner by the best poker hand or by the total points on the cards.

Equipment Needed for Practice

Every cross country coach should have access to the tools of the trade to conduct a practice. The following is a list of equipment you should have access to.

- **Cones.** I keep at least 24 of them in my car and use them frequently. For drills to learn pace on the track, put a cone at every 100-meter mark. When you call out splits, the athletes can judge whether they are running an even pace. Almost every workout requires cones. You can usually find them at a sporting goods store.
- **Small flags.** I use three colors. Red means stay right, blue means stay left, and yellow means either side. You can find these at a home improvement or hardware store.
- **Wheel.** You need a metric measuring wheel that you can roll on the ground to measure distances to ensure accuracy. Take it to course rehearsals and measure off areas near the start and finish so you can practice them.
- **Poles with reflector lights.** These are good for marking corners if you are creating a course and need visual cues for runners to find their way.
- **Stopwatches (3-4).** These are for timing intervals. When you have more than one group running at a time, you may need assistants to pitch in.
- **GPS watches.** Modern watches that have bells and whistles chart the distance, location, and time.
- **Water.** Five-gallon (about 20 L) jugs work well. You also need disposable cups and a garbage sack.
- **First-aid kit.** This is a tool box or tackle box containing all of the things you might need for simple first aid. If a kid carries medication for bee sting allergies, or needs an inhaler nearby, store it here. The trainer or nurse usually keeps the box stocked with things like white medical tape, adhesive strips, gauze, scissors, petroleum jelly, disinfectant, and antibacterial spray or ointment. This is a good place for spike wrenches and spikes in a variety of sizes.
- **Batons.** Carry these in the first-aid kit in case they're needed for a relay.
- **Popsicles.** Have a cooler handy if it's a hot day early in the season.
- **Cell phone.** You never know when you might need to make a call in case of an emergency.
- **Video camera.** There are times when you might want to evaluate form and technique.
- **Laptop computer or tablet.** Have this nearby if you want to show a motivational video, or need access to information or data. Many coaches use tablets to record video also.
- **Clipboard and pencil.** It seems like there is always something on paper that you might want or need to read to the team, such as the workout plan or notes that you don't want to forget. If you take roll, you can have the roster handy on the clipboard.

Positive Feedback: Concluding Practice

At the close of practice, reinforce the value of what just happened. Review the workout, and tell the athletes what a great job they did. Tell them you're excited about their progress. If the workout fell short of expectations or had other problems, mention what could have gone better, but be sure come back and try to put a bow on it. I never wanted a kid who had given an effort to walk away from practice disappointed or frustrated. For that reason, practice should always end on a positive note. This is also a time to review what's coming the rest of the week, to go over the logistics of the next bus trip. Remind the kids what they need to do to be prepared for the next week. Conclude whatever you say with energy. Tell your runners to keep their commitment, keep writing in their journals, and to be inspired. I sometimes wrapped it up with an inspirational quote from John Wooden or someone else. And sometimes I surprised them by cracking open the cooler and revealing the Popsicles.

Summary

Practice is a great time of day because it's when your team is unified on the goal of getting better and preparing for the next race, both physically and emotionally. It's possible to have fun at practice and also get a lot of serious work done.

- Athletes should come to practice mentally prepared for the workout, focused and ready to enjoy themselves and support their teammates.

- A morning run is a great way to begin the day, clear the head, get the heart pumping, and tack on a few extra miles.
- SGP—stretching, gut-busters, push-ups—is indispensable for becoming flexible, tough, and strong.
- Weight lifting might be appealing as complementary training to build strength, but it's not necessary during the season.
- Don't be afraid to put away the watch. If it's windy, if your athletes have colds, or if everybody is worn down, put the stopwatch away and focus on the value of effort.
- Games are a great way to switch gears, have fun, be competitive, and run with excitement.
- Have on hand all of the tools that you might need to conduct practice.

PART III

TEACHING TECHNIQUES AND TACTICS

Teaching Proper Running Form

The ongoing effort to train young athletes, to make them faster and stronger, is also tied to the way they run. Perfect running form is elusive and even the best distance runners in the world look for tiny tweaks they can make that might help them improve by a few seconds.

One hundred runners on a high school cross country team might run with 100 different styles, some more pleasing to watch, not to mention more efficient, than others. But in general, our bodies tend to move in the ways that make us feel most comfortable. As coaches, it is our job to coax athletes in the direction of better form as a way to run faster and reduce injuries. At the elite level, form flaws and other slight imbalances can be the difference between an injury-free season and a stress fracture. That can also be true at the high school level.

In this chapter I go into detail about stride length, proper arm action, and other efficiency issues that come up in every program. And I offer tips to help young runners with their mechanics, including strength exercises to improve overall running form. Two key workouts that I've used to focus on proper form are the Oregon drill and Joaquim Cruz circuits.

Proper Technique

You want to identify several key elements of effective running form right away. You want your athletes to run tall, with a long, upright posture that maximizes the length of their levers and opens up the lungs (see figure 7.1). That said, you don't want them to look unnaturally rigid or tight, either. You want them tall but also relaxed.

FIGURE 7.1 Running tall.

I tell kids to carry a feather between their index finger and thumb. This promotes the idea of running light and loose. You don't want tension in their arms and hands. But you also don't want hands and wrists that are floppy (see figure 7.2).

Arms should be held no higher than the shoulders and no lower than the hips (see figure 7.3). Most kids have a natural arm motion that is comfortable, and I tended not to correct it unless it became a problem. The

FIGURE 7.2 Loose hands.

FIGURE 7.3 Good arm motion.

thing to watch for is tightness in the arm carriage. It's a sign that the athlete is carrying tension and needs to loosen up.

High Speed

Proper running form, arm carriage, and upright posture are easy to maintain at a jogging pace. It's much more difficult at the end of the 5,000 meters when you are trying to lift and sprint as hard as possible.

As a coach, you want kids to be strong enough to run fast even when they are tired. On top of that, you want them to run fast and remain relaxed. Focusing on arms to drive the legs with a little more gusto can be a big help at the end of a race. Powerful arm drive coming down the homestretch and relaxation in the face are sure signs of closing strong.

Hills

The best way to run hills is to slightly lean into them, pushing the center of gravity out front. My rule of thumb is "nose ahead of toes." Also, runners should rise onto their toes, which tends to happen naturally if they are leaning into the slope. Occasionally, you might want your athletes to attack hills in order to gain ground on the opposition or pull away. But in general, my advice is "pace it, don't race it." Otherwise, there's no energy left at the top of the hill. Strong, active arms can be helpful going up.

Coming down the hill, the foot strike naturally transitions from the toes to the heels. It's the first place the ground makes contact with the foot. Reaching out with the feet and lengthening the stride will help to gain more ground and prevent any tendency to lean back into the hill. Leaning back will apply a braking force to the running stride, which will slow the runner down. Runners should use their arms in a normal fashion but carry them a little lower. Runners should let things go a little bit on the downhills as long as they can remain in control. This is a place on the course where they don't want to hold back unless there are hazards or concerns about falling. Gravity is their friend.

Arm Swing and Racing Stride

At race pace, a runner should strive for efficient short strides that are dictated by arm movement. Generally, the hands move down to the hip and back up near shoulder height. The arm swing is smooth and concise. Watch a video of Matthew Centrowitz, Galen Rupp, or Shalane Flanagan, three current athletes who have efficient strides and arm motion.

Running hills and stairs can help make a stride more efficient by training the muscles to generate more power in each stride. Generally, the legs will follow the arms. Short efficient arms will create an efficient stride and prevent over striding. A longer, more powerful arm swing will open up a stride, helping to create a longer sprinting stride useful at the end of a race.

Foot Strike

Aim for midfoot or ball-of-the-foot contact with the ground. An athlete who runs on the front half of the foot goes faster. Landing on the heels and rolling from back to front is a slower process and less efficient. Instead, runners want to feel a little bouncy and frisky. Again, hill running is a great way to promote running on the toes.

Athletes who run on their toes are pushers, lightly pushing themselves away and forward from the surface. Runners who are less bouncy and make contact farther back are pullers. Some excellent runners are shufflers who fit into this category, and sometimes biomechanics dictate one style over the other. But in general, the pusher is faster than the puller.

Common Mistakes

A few easy-to-spot technique flaws can be corrected. If runners overstride and take long loping steps, it usually means that they are not swinging the hands in a hip-to-shoulder motion. Many young runners carry their arms from side to side, which sometimes is caused by a lack of upper-body strength. Running drills, push-ups, pull-ups, and the strength exercises in chapter 6 can remedy this problem.

Some differences in gait and running form you'll just have to live with. No two people run exactly the same. Some runners don't run tall, and usually that's a sign of weak hips. They tend to look seated while running. Ask them to keep their hips elevated and to think tall. The stretching drills in chapter 6 help to strengthen the hips, and again, uphill running will improve running form.

Technique Drills

The following drills promote speed and relaxation as well as correct running form, including arm action and posture.

SPRINT, FLOAT, SPRINT

This drill practices closing in the late stage of a race, whether it's on the track or on a cross country course. It begins 150 meters from the finish line. Set up cones at the 150-, 100-, and 50-meter marks.

The first 50 is a sprint. The second 50 is a float in which the runner focuses on relaxing the face and arms. The pace backs off just a tad and the focus is relaxation. The final 50 is a sprint through the finish line (see figure 7.4).

The runner focuses on driving the elbows back for more power and to find another gear without losing control. This drill is meant to instill an automatic response over the final 150, to find one more crank without becoming unhinged. During the last 150 meters, form is more important than at any other time in a race. This is a drill you might use at the end of a course rehearsal, practicing to pass opposing runners and finish with a flourish.

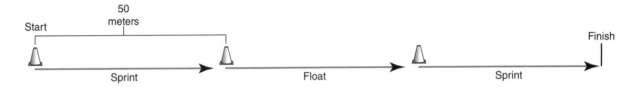

FIGURE 7.4 Sprint, float, sprint setup.

1,600 METERS

Beginning at the start of the backstretch (the 300 mark), run 500 meters at whatever pace you assign, followed by a 400-meter jog, a 400-meter interval, a 300-meter jog, a 300-meter interval, a 200-meter jog, a 200-meter interval, a 100-meter jog, and a 100-meter sprint, and one final 100-meter jog and 100-meter sprint that brings the runner to the finish line. The totals of the interval distances add up to 1,600 meters. With each timed interval, the pace becomes progressively faster. This drill teaches runners about pace and how to adjust it while on the move.

OREGON DRILL

This drill, which I also described in chapter 5, was originally devised as a rehab running drill for Oregon athletes coming back from injury, but at Mead I found it was also a great way to work on mechanics. This is a meat-and-potatoes staple that serves several purposes. First, we do it barefoot and on grass. (Form issues tend to become more apparent with shoes off). Second, it's simple to set up. Use cones to designate three running lanes that are about 20 meters wide and 80 meters long. This would be end zone to end zone if it's on a football field. You want one lane along each sideline and one through the middle (see figure 7.5).

The first lane is for easy pace. The middle lane is for medium, or cross country race pace, and the third lane is for a gradual pick-up to closing sprint speed. Runners jog slowly the 20 meters between cones to switch lanes. When runners complete the third lane, they jog easily back to the start and repeat the progression. Run this drill for 30 minutes nonstop. At the end of the season, as we were tuning up for the state championship, we ran this for 20 minutes.

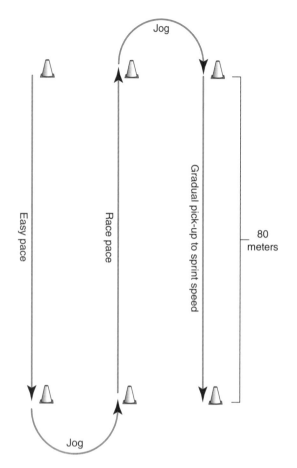

FIGURE 7.5 Oregon drill setup.

While the athletes are running, watch or even videotape the workout. Break the overall group into smaller packs of five or six. The Oregon drill is free flowing and requires minimal input. Use this time to analyze the form of the runners and take notes about deficiencies you might see. This drill incorporates fartlek with its speed changes, which allows you to analyze form and how it changes from one gear to the next. Review this information with the runners through video or make critiques as you watch.

JOAQUIM CRUZ CIRCUITS

Joaquim Cruz was a Brazilian middle-distance runner who competed for Oregon in the early 1980s and developed into the best 800-meter runner in the world. After doubling in the 800 and 1,500 meters at the 1984 NCAA championships and winning both races, he qualified for the Olympics in Los Angeles and won the gold medal in the 800.

This drill is adapted from something that Cruz did in college. He was a soccer player growing up, so he incorporated agility drills into his running training, which evolved into a continuous circuit of exercises. He jogged, sprinted, did jumping jacks and push-ups, and sprinted again, always moving without rest until every step was completed. I did not do this regularly during cross country season, maybe just once or twice, but it fit into the principle of variation. It broke up the training cycle and prevented it from becoming stale.

The value of this exercise can be measured several ways. Agility and flexibility are woven into the circuit, both of which help promote correct running form. It includes high knees, butt kicks, and other drills from the warm-up routine. And it includes elements of running tall, quick arms, and the proper arm action that brings the hands from the shoulder to the hip.

You can arrange the circuit many ways, but you want to set it up to roll from one thing to the next without varying the intensity. Move from something difficult to something medium to something easy and repeat.

1. Jog 10 minutes
2. Jumping jack × 20
3. Stride 100 meters
4. Twister × 20
5. Stride 100 meters
6. Squat thrust × 10
7. Stride 100 meters
8. High knee × 20
9. Stride 100 meters
10. Leg lunge × 10
11. Stride 100 meters
12. Push-up × 20
13. Stride 100 meters
14. Butt kick × 20
15. Stride 100 meters
16. Twist sit-up × 10
17. Stride 100 meters
18. Sprint 100 meters
19. Jog 5 minutes

Perform three or four sets. You can vary the circuit by using different distances, stadium stairs, and so on. Following are brief descriptions of the exercises.

Jumping jack: With feet together and arms at side, jump to a position with feet spread wide and hands touching overhead. Jump again and return to the start position (see figure 7.6).

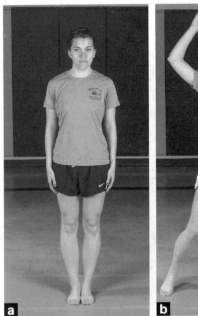

FIGURE 7.6 Jumping jack.

Twister: Twist the torso in one direction and then the other (see figure 7.7).

FIGURE 7.7   Twister.

Squat thrust: Bend at the knees into a squat position (see figure 7.8*a*). Then put hands on the ground and jump legs back into a push-up position (see figure 7.8*b*). Jump back into a squat and then stand up straight.

FIGURE 7.8   Squat thrust.

High knee: Exaggerate knee lift so that when the knee is lifted in front, it is bent to a 90-degree angle (see figure 7.9). The hip should also reach a 90-degree angle.

FIGURE 7.9   High knee.

> *continued*

Leg lunge: Take a step forward, bend at the knee, and dip low until the trailing knee is a few inches (5 cm) off the ground (see figure 7.10). Stand up straight and step forward with the opposite leg.

FIGURE 7.10 Leg lunge.

Push-up: Keep back straight and press until arms are straight (see figure 7.11).

FIGURE 7.11 Push-up.

Butt kick: Exaggerate leg lift behind so that the heel makes contact with rear end (see figure 7.12).

FIGURE 7.12 Butt kick.

Twist sit-up: Use abdominals to lift torso off the ground and twist one way, then the other on the next rep (see figure 7.13).

FIGURE 7.13 Twist sit-up.

Running Barefoot

I almost always had athletes do the Oregon drill barefoot. It's an opportunity to take the shoes and socks off and run on a nice lush surface. But I also did this drill to break in new racing spikes before a big meet like state.

I was at a Stanford camp and heard Olympic runner PattiSue Plumer talk about a barefoot component to training. She said you need strong feet to become less injury prone. One hundred years ago—and for centuries—kids played outside without shoes. They ran and jumped and played games, and they had calluses on their feet. I think there is an important link between running barefoot and form, as well. It tends to promote running on the ball of the foot instead of the heel. Running on the heel seems to be a byproduct of wearing shoes with thick cushioning in the back.

I believe running barefoot makes your feet stronger and helps prevent injuries. I can't cite scientific studies on this, but I can tell you from experience that there is something invigorating and toughening about incorporating 20 to 30 minutes a week of barefoot running if you have a safe, comfortable grass or synthetic turf field. It's a treat, like a massage of the tendons and ligaments of the foot.

However, I advise against racing barefoot. I never had an athlete who wanted to do this, but I probably wouldn't have let him. I'd be concerned that rocks, glass, sticks, pine cones, or something else sharp might cause a problem that could have been easily prevented by wearing shoes.

Teaching Tools

Flawed running form is generally caused by biomechanical imbalances, weaknesses, or inflexibility in certain muscle groups. Everybody has them, and it is important to remember that some difference in running gait between individuals is natural.

Developing overall fitness is important for proper technique. The stretches, gutbusters, push-ups, and weightlifting exercises mentioned in chapter 6 may help to improve any biomechanical weaknesses runners may have. Building upper-body and arm strength can improve a runner's arm action. The arm swing is a vital component to creating an efficient and powerful racing stride.

Videotaping your runners is also a great way to show them what they can't see for themselves. This is a great tool for helping runners understand what running tall should look like. Ideally, the line between the shoulders and hips should be perpendicular to the ground while running on a flat surface. Another way for runners to subtly learn to perfect their craft is by pairing them with other runners who already exhibit good form. Runners may adjust their technique subconsciously to match.

I was careful not to criticize any high school student's form or make them feel like they need to reinvent the wheel. I preferred to keep it simple by focusing on helping my runners build strength and flexibility, ease tension in the shoulders and hands, and use their arms correctly.

Summary

Instruction on running form and mechanics is important but can also be tricky. Every kid runs a little differently, but small adjustments to arm carriage, posture, and foot strike can lead to marked improvement and also prevent injuries.

- Although each runner moves in a different way, there are general guidelines for improving form and technique. Better running form can lead to better performance and fewer injuries.

- The first step in achieving proper running form is to ask athletes to run tall.

- When running up hills, athletes should lean slightly into the slope and push off with the front of the foot. When coming down, they should let gravity help but should stay in control.

- Correct arm carriage is a big part of efficiency, and arms can also drive the finishing sprint.

- A forefoot plant is more desirable than a heel strike for producing speed.

- Several drills promote relaxation while running at a fast tempo, address weaknesses, and allow for coaches' evaluation.

- Barefoot running can help improve form because it promotes staying on the ball of the foot and also strengthens and toughens the foot.

CHAPTER 8 | Improving Runners' Performance

In this chapter, we take a closer look at one of the five principles we've already discussed more thoroughly: progression. Young runners constantly look for ways to get a little better, to drop a few more seconds. Few things in cross country are more satisfying than a personal record, and that's a goal that is attainable for every runner who goes to the starting line of a race. As a coach, you can set up your athletes to succeed by helping them understand the pace they run now and the pace they want to get to. Also, uninterrupted progress means limiting injuries and managing them correctly. And there's no greater key to avoiding injury than communication.

Using Date Pace and Goal Pace

An athlete's current speed is his or her date pace and there is no guesswork involved. Date pace comes from the most recent race or time trial and establishes a baseline. It's where an athlete is now. Goal pace could be derived from date pace or it could be established independently, but it is a reasonable, attainable expectation of where an athlete will be at the end of the season.

A freshman, for example, should not set a goal pace so far ahead of date pace that he or she might not reach it until senior year. Goal pace should be reasonably attainable within the current season, and it can be adjusted. If progress is rapid and date pace surpasses goal pace, the coach and athlete need to reevaluate and set a new benchmark to strive for. You may find that you are constantly readjusting goal pace for rookies, and that's great. Beating one goal and moving onto the next is what cross country is all about. If you have a freshman girl who ran 21 minutes in her first time trial of the season, you might set a very attainable goal of 20:30 (1:38 for 400, 4:05 for 1,000 and 6:35 per mile). She may go past that in a matter of weeks, but you can always set a new benchmark when she does. Experience will dial you in to selecting goal paces for veteran runners and helping them to push the envelope. In the meantime, err on conservative goal paces with your rookies.

Let's use 18 minutes flat for 5,000 meters at a preseason time trial as a starting point for determining a sophomore boy's goal pace. It means he ran 200 meters at a rate of 43 seconds. For 400, it's 86 seconds. For 800, it's 2:53. For 1,000 meters, it's 3:36, and for 1,600 meters it's 5:45. Now, let's say that his goal is to run 5,000 meters in 17:20. His goal pace is 41.5 for 200 meters, 83 for 400, 2:46 for 800, 3:28 for 1,000, and 5:33 for 1,600 meters.

These numbers inform the targets he wants to hit during intervals at practice. Right after establishing a new date pace, an athlete will stick primarily to that pace but also include one or two intervals at goal pace. It's a way for the athlete to feel the difference. Over time, the athlete will make incremental adjustments and do more of the workout at goal pace than date pace. And the progress should be evident during races, although cross country courses are typically not comparable.

Let's say that every athlete on the team has been through the first race and has a date pace to work with, as well as a goal pace. In a workout of 5 × 1,000-meter intervals, the athlete who ran 18:00 should do the first, third, and fifth intervals at date pace (3:36) with a 2:00 recovery. The second and fourth intervals should employ goal pace (3:28) with a little more recovery, maybe 2:30. This gives the athlete a chance to touch base with his goal. You can do that workout on a track or by measuring a 1,000-meter loop on grass.

When a motivated athlete is rolling, the goals become more and more ambitious.

Later, with this same workout, the athlete may switch to goal pace on the first, third, and fifth intervals and date pace on the second and fourth. But this time, you may cut the recovery time down. By the end of the season, nearly everything should be at goal pace. If the athlete were doing 200s, he'd start with 43 seconds for date pace and 41.5 for goal pace.

At the next meet, the athlete hopefully gets a little faster. And the date pace improves accordingly. Over time, you want to assign more volume at goal pace and also do it with less recovery to simulate race conditions.

The same principles go into a workout like the 30-30 drill. The athlete runs at goal pace for 30 seconds, jogs for 30 seconds to recover, and repeats. This is a good workout to help an athlete not only touch base with goal pace but also to understand what it takes to arrive at a goal time at the end of the season.

Goal Setting

Once you've got a team rolling, you know what you have to do. But when you are establishing a team, stated goals are more important. With a new situation, it's important to sit down with the team and discuss the mission.

Based on what happened the previous year, how high do you set the bar? Perhaps you got fourth out of eight in the league and everybody is back. You should be in the hunt for the league title. What's it going to take? Get them to believe they're going to do their part. Ask them: What's your contribution to the team this year?

Goal setting can also happen in one-on-one conferences with the athletes. You might say to a runner, "You were the sixth man last year and two of the guys ahead of you have graduated. Do you see yourself as the No. 4 next fall or No. 1?" This sort of discussion keeps athletes accountable. What are they going to contribute?

There are many types of goals. Maybe it's as simple as being on time for practice every day. Maybe it's to get a varsity letter. Maybe it's to help the team win the league championship or qualify for state. If it's an exceptional athlete, he or she might look toward a state title or a berth at Foot Locker. Maybe the goal is a time. If an athlete wants to run 16:30, explain what that means. That's 5:20 per mile, 80 seconds per quarter. Reinforce the goal by stating it back, "I like what you are going to contribute to the team. That 16:30 you are aiming for could put you right in our mix for a top-seven spot."

It doesn't matter how talented a runner is, there is a goal out there for everybody. The goal could be to show up every day and run. It could be a personal challenge to improve from 10:00 per mile to 9:00. That's progress. I once had a kid who lost 75 pounds (34 kg) in the three years he was at Mead, and he became a 1:56 800-meter runner (see chapter 13). Every team has more kids like that than they do superstars trying to make it to Nike Cross Nationals or Foot Locker.

The top-end athletes that you are fortunate to have are usually totally committed to the process. They have big goals that don't usually need to be spelled out. They know they want to be a state champions. They know they want to qualify for nationals. They know the tradition, and they don't want to let down the jersey.

The bottom line is that there are many ways to win in cross country. When kids score new personal bests, they win self-esteem. When kids put in the work to get into better shape, they win their health. When kids put effort into being supportive members of a team, they win friends. A great deal of this book is geared toward building a championship team, but for the vast majority of high school distance runners, participation in cross country is not defined by winning the race. Instead, it's incremental self-improvement, day by day, on all fronts.

Navigating a Midseason Slump

Sometimes the momentum of a season slows. The energy wanes and it's difficult for the kids to stay positively charged. As a coach, you may notice it in a practice or even a race. It could be one athlete or the whole lot, and the slump is usually caused by fatigue, whether physical, mental, or emotional. You may have lined up workouts in a way that was too ambitious, and the athletes are tired. Perhaps they are staying up too late at night working on projects or studying for tests. Maybe another stress is affecting members of the team.

I always tried to identify the signs of a slump coming before it happened. And my first inclination was always to go back to basics. That meant coming in to talk to the guys before practice and changing the plan. We found a trail with inspiring scenery and ran free and loose and felt the air in our lungs. The purpose was to go out and change the script and come back feeling refreshed.

It's the same with an individual who has hit a wall. Find a way to let the athlete know that it's OK to take a break, get necessary rest, and find a way to reboot. Help that person find the fun in cross country again. You can also avoid an oncoming slump by canceling the workout and choosing to play a game instead or planning a pizza party or barbeque after practice. Variation is the spice of life.

Getting Athletes to Tell You What's Wrong

In 1993, after smashing the course record at our state championship, Matt Davis was running at Manito Park when he slipped on ice and torqued his IT band.

He came to me immediately and told me what had happened and how his knee felt. My first suggestion was that he have it checked out by his doctor, which he did. But we also had a discussion about whether he should continue to run on the injury or shut down his training and skip the postseason Foot Locker West Regional and Foot Locker Championships races. Matt insisted he could push through it. "I'm a senior. Let's go for it," he said. Fortunately, he also got a green light from his doctor. So we proceeded, with caution, and he ran well in both races.

I can't overstate the importance of communication between athlete and coach when it comes to pain, discomfort, illness, or any other health issue. If an athlete persists when hurt and keeps his or her condition from you, it's only going to get worse. And that can be a challenge. Lots of high school runners are inclined to tough it out or suck it up and try to press on. A spot on varsity may be at stake. The chance to help a team win an important meet could be on the line.

As a coach, though, you have to know what's going on so you can make informed decisions and do what's right for the individual and the team. It's important to build trust and free-flowing communication with athletes so that they don't feel threatened by divulging their aches and pains to you.

You want kids to tell you, "My knee's bothering me," or "My Achilles aches." And you need to make them understand how important it is for you to know when those problems crop up. If you have an athlete walking around in pain, it may require a week of rest or more to make it stop. If he or she continues to push, the danger is that the injury will become more severe. But when you, the coach, know what's going on, you can manage it. You can suggest ways to cross-train so that the athlete's fitness remains intact while resting the injury.

Managing Injuries

When an athlete comes to you and says, "I've got pain in my shin," it's important to know how to respond. I immediately suggested ice and ibuprofen. I also automatically suggested the athlete run on a soft surface. And I checked to make sure his shoes fit correctly. I told him I would back down the intensity of the workout. He could either run with a slower group or run in his usual group but do less. There were a mix of options, but I erred on the side of doing less. If the pain persisted, I shut him down completely and asked him to see his doctor.

You can suggest doing less or cross-training to keep the heart rate up to avoid losing hard-won fitness. But when you can look at an athlete and feel the pain or notice a limp, there is nothing else to do; he or she is done running until their injury is healed. If you don't take that precaution, a stress reaction could easily lead to a debilitating stress fracture. When pain persists, make sure the athlete

(or more directly, the parents) seek out great sports medicine doctors or trainers to get their expert opinions. It's not an easy decision to have one of your runners sit out while the rest of the team goes on, but you have to think about the future health and happiness of the athlete. There are many more years and racing opportunities ahead.

In addition to stress reactions and fractures, the most common injuries for cross country runners are located in the iliotibial (IT) band attachment in the knee, the plantar fascia in the bottom of the foot, and the Achilles tendon. Knee or hip pain is commonly caused by irritation in the growth plate in the knee (called Osgood-Schlatter disease). Following are common injuries among cross country runners.

- **Stress reaction.** Persistent pain in the tibia is commonly diagnosed as a stress reaction. If it goes untreated, it can advance to a stress fracture, which is one of the more common overuse injuries that affect runners. Depending on where you are in the season, I would be cautious but also work with the athlete to see whether it's possible to keep running. A doctor's appointment is always a good idea, especially when you know you are dealing with something serious.

- **Plantar fasciitis.** Simply put, this is an inflammation of the thick tissue on the bottom of the foot. The soreness caused by this inflammation lingers and can be debilitating. Plantar fasciitis is difficult to overcome because it can take a long time to heal. Deep-tissue massage is an effective remedy, and there are tools to help accelerate the recovery: foam rollers, hard rollers, and ropes, to name a few. But more than anything, plantar fasciitis requires rest and time off.

- **Achilles tendon pain.** With the Achilles, sometimes the irritation or pain will go away quickly if the athlete stops abusing it. Athletes with Achilles tendinitis should stay away from hills and refrain from intervals, where they are more likely to run on their toes. Runners should stay on soft surfaces and avoid aggravating or straining the affected area. It's also helpful to treat the area with a bag of ice or frozen peas after a workout.

- **Knee and hip pain.** This is often associated with growth plate problems and is usually best dealt with by holding the athlete out of practices. When there is pain in both hips or both knees, chances are it is, indeed, a growth plate problem. And that's OK. As a high school cross country coach, you will have athletes who are growing and maturing rapidly. The stresses of running and the body's natural growth—in some case inches in height over a matter of a few months—don't always go well together. Massage is a great treatment, but sometimes time off is required. There's no sense in trying to outwit Mother Nature.

Shadowing Excellence

When athletes place limits on their possibilities, it can stunt their progress. I want kids who aren't afraid to dream big. That's why I've always tried to demonstrate what a higher level looks like and feels like. But you don't have to take a busload of kids to the national cross country championships or the Olympic Trials to see excellence. All you have to do is create situations where your top seven have a chance to model excellence for younger or slower runners.

There are times when it's not only appropriate but also necessary to move runners from the comfort zone of a slower group into the mix with a faster group. The experience of going on a run with the top runners in your school and of learning to explore new possibilities is the way some kids get better.

If kids gets stuck in the C-level group and become complacent, their progress may stall. It's better to give every member of the team the opportunity to make gradual progress by being able to work out with better runners. For the sake of the program and its continuity from one season to the next, it's imperative. It's also a good reason to have an assistant with serious running chops. A mid-20s guy out of college with superior talent and racing experience can give even your No. 1 someone to chase.

Shadowing excellence often involves younger runners following the example of older runners. Here, senior Evan Garber (937) leads the 2003 Washington state meet with Laef Barnes not far behind.

Hamburger to Sirloin at Oregon

All any University of Oregon runner wanted to do was please Bill Bowerman, and it was no easy task. In the rare moment he did acknowledge my presence, he called me Tim. So when he approached me one day in the spring of 1969, my freshman year, and suggested that I might be better suited as team manager, I was crushed.

I didn't go to Oregon to pay my tuition and not run. So I buckled down and continued to shadow some of the top runners on the team, but I was still on the outside of the elite club. Bowerman owned a herd of cattle and he sometimes spoke of his runners in terms any cattleman would understand. I was "hamburger" and the older, more accomplished guys were "sirloin." I had a good work ethic. I showed up on time and kept my mouth shut.

During that long first year, I wrote a couple of letters to Rick Riley at Washington State. I cherished his advice. I sent him letters telling him how I was doing and asked him a couple of questions. And to my amazement, he always wrote back.

Truthfully, I entertained thoughts about transferring after Bowerman's suggestion that I consider becoming the manager. That spring I also had a stress fracture, which didn't help. The old coach never gave me any sympathy. He figured that I'd probably never make it.

I went home to Tacoma over the summer and got back into training and went to a couple of meets in the area. And I got better. When I returned to Eugene in the fall, freshman Steve Prefontaine immediately became the cross country team's No. 1. I worked my way up to No. 8. I started to gain more respect. I began to feel like part of the club. Bowerman gave me little attention, and he never mentioned the manager position again.

In the spring, I was close to earning a chance to wear the Oregon jersey in the first track meet of the season. But then I was in an accident. I was riding my bicycle on campus when a car door swung open and hit me, knocking me to the road. None of my injuries were serious, but I missed the opportunity to run in that first dual meet. I redshirted that season. I ran in meets unattached and set new personal records. I ran 14 minutes flat for three miles, and I consistently broke 9:00 for two miles. I could break 30:00 for six miles.

In the fall of 1970, I made the varsity cross country team and was the No. 6 man. We placed second in the NCAA meet. I was on the traveling team with guys like Pre, Randy James, and Steve Savage. I was finally sirloin, not hamburger.

In the spring of 1971, I competed in a few meets and I won the three mile in our dual meet against rival Oregon State, if only because the top two finishers were disqualified for elbowing one another. The following cross country season was exciting. We placed third out of four teams in the Northern Division and second at the Pac-8 Championships. Ten days later, we won the NCAA Championship in Knoxville, Tennessee. Pre won, of course, and I was our No. 3 runner, 31st overall.

Less than two months later, I moved into the trailer with Pre and became his roommate. Living with him and shadowing his excellence, I continued to evolve. At the Pac-8 Championships that spring, I competed alongside my roommate in the three mile. Pre won it. I was third. We got the team 16 points. The rest of the team had not competed well, and Bowerman was not a happy camper. But he found me and said, "I'm proud of what you did today." Those words changed things for me. I became someone that Bowerman could rely on. He asked me to attend booster club meetings and luncheons, where I stood up to speak on behalf of the team.

I ran in the six miles at the 1972 NCAA Championships but didn't finish high enough to score. I qualified for the Olympic Trials in that event, too, but was injured again and wasn't able to run. In the fall of 1972, in my last season of cross country, I was sometimes our No. 1. We finished third at the NCAA championships.

I knew, deep down, that running with guys who were better than me, by shadowing excellence, I got stronger and gained more confidence. Over time, you become better equipped to handle the stress of an intense pace because you taste it on a regular basis with your teammates.

Summary

There are no magic formulas for getting better, and it certainly doesn't happen overnight. By carefully managing workouts and explaining their purpose, you can help your runners see progress and know where their trajectory is headed.

- Progression in cross country comes from each runner understanding the difference between date pace and goal pace and taking the necessary steps to make the incremental adjustment from one to the other.

- Goal pace is the target that each runner aims to achieve. Races serve to reestablish individual benchmarks and set new date paces.

- Athletes must understand the importance of being forthcoming and communicative about injuries. It's another reason it's important to establish trust. Coaches should also watch for signs of pain in an athlete's face or limping.

- Shins, Achilles tendons, feet, knees, and hips are all areas commonly affected by the rigors of cross country training. Coaches must manage injuries carefully so that they don't get worse.

- Every athlete should have a chance to see an elite-level or college race in order to see what the sport looks like at a higher level. Also, every athlete should be allowed to dream big and learn something along the way from older or faster runners. In this way, each member of the team has an opportunity to shadow excellence.

Developing a Race Strategy

The strategy of a cross country race is simple: You want to put more of your runners ahead of their runners at the finish line. Lowest score wins. Sure, running in a pack during a race can be a great advantage, but only if that pack is moving fast. When it comes to racing strategy, I believe in keeping it simple. If you've put in quality work in practice, prepared mentally for the challenge of the race, and studied the course, you should be ready to roll. I'm not much into overthinking the race.

Balancing Coaching and Freedom

I believe in giving a long leash to the athletes. When I got to Mead, I had a new guy coming in named Chris Lewis. He was a thoroughbred. He ate up the workouts. In fact, it was like he was racing in practice, which is something that most of the time you want to avoid as a coach.

On the track, he'd try some radical things. He'd run the first half of a 1,600-meter race in 1:58, or run the first half of a 3,200 meters in 4:18 when he'd never broke 9:00 for the full race distance before. I decided to let him go, but I also took a little bit of heat for it. "Why aren't you teaching him about pace?" someone would ask. My response was, "Well, why not let him go until he gets beat?"

Letting them go so they can explore and test their instincts is an idea worth considering. Lewis was a five-time state champion (including two cross country titles). He ran nation-leading times in the 1,600 meters (4:04.06) and 3,200 meters (8:50.65) in the spring of 1989. A local newspaper writer at the time had a line that I loved. He said Chris "looked like an altar boy and ran like the devil."

He personified my early teams at Mead, which were filled with guys who ran hard and then ran even harder. They didn't worry about their splits. They didn't care about strategy. These guys ran for the intoxicating feeling of an all-out effort. Maybe it was because I was feeding them stories about Pre. Whatever it was, we relished it. At the 1988 state meet, Lewis blasted out of the gate and went through his first mile in 4:30. It was 38 seconds faster than the first mile the previous year. It was less about strategy than it was about being aggressive and testing his limits.

I have never been particularly interested in devising race strategies. At Mead, our guys didn't purposely run behind our opponents, waiting to kick past them at the end. They didn't choose to run slow on one part of the course and pick another spot to go fast. Instead, we tried to run honest and run with heart. If that flies in the face of conventional wisdom, then so be it.

Runners eventually get the hang of what racing is all about. If they go out too fast, they'll learn what the consequences are and make the adjustment. And as you build a culture within your program, you will find that information is passed down from one class to the next. The younger runners always have questions for older runners. What's it like at state? Are you nervous? What happened behind those trees when we couldn't see you in the dual against Ferris? How did you decide when it was the right time to kick? And the veterans, the seniors, have the answers: This is what you do and this is how you do it.

A cross country race isn't an orchestra and it isn't rocket science. It's just running. The simpler you keep it, the better. When you think about it too much, you complicate the game. The race is a set distance and fits into a specific time window. At Mead, and for most high schools in the U.S., that was 5,000 meters and 16 to 17 minutes. Ideally, two days before a race, you should conduct a rehearsal of the course. On meet day, the energy is already high. There is no need to be in the way.

I used the Oregon workout ideas and that hard-easy pattern discussed in chapter 5 and tried to make it fun, make it exciting. When you use those principles and include variety in your training and in your racing, then strategy boils down to doing what you can do to be the best you can be.

I didn't need to tell my teams who to look out for in a race. I didn't need to tell them where to surge or where to try to relax and conserve energy. Your runners learn these

On race day, runners do their best to test the limits of their fitness, but nothing beats experience for learning how to be a better racer.

things on their own from workouts, from talking to teammates, and from experience. Young runners may reveal their personalities in their race performance, going too aggressively or too conservatively. That's OK. Over time, experience will correct those flaws and teach them how to expend their energy more effectively. All I said to my teams was, "Be sure you have enough jelly beans at the end of the race. Don't eat them all in the first mile."

Keeping It Simple

At Mead, the race plan was typically the same every time and it was basic: Go out hard. Take charge. Have fun. We attributed those words to a runner we had named Matt Zweifel. He was killed in a car accident the summer before his junior year, and he was on his way to becoming one of the top guys on the team. He coined the saying "Go out hard. Take charge. Have fun." and after he died, it became our battle cry and carried extra significance because of who he was and how much we missed him. But those seven words carry a lot of information related to race strategy, so let's look at them more closely.

The first mile, go out hard and put yourself in a nice position. Take charge in the second mile, meaning stay alert and keep attacking while everyone else is relaxing. Have fun in the third mile; pass a few people if you can and finish with a rush. Tell yourself you're not tired and that you have one more gear.

Learning the mentality of each athlete is one of the fascinating aspects of coaching. You will learn over time what makes each one tick. "Go out hard; take charge; have fun" may be a rally cry that doesn't apply to every runner, like the one who prefers to hang in the back at the start and then try to move up later. Some guys like to show off and jump out in front of a race recklessly. I would caution them by saying never take the lead in a race unless you know you are going to win. But even in a situation like that, I would err on the side of letting the kid be a free spirit in his or her own race strategy. Race experience usually makes runners smarter.

Overcoming Self-Doubt

Some kids tie themselves up in knots before and during races because they think too much. And most of the time it is worry and self-doubt. I know this because I used to be one of those kids. Remember, it was Prefontaine who told me to stop being a worrywart.

We had a runner at Mead named Greg Kuntz, who was a talented guy, but he was also overburdened with self-doubt. Getting him to clear his head and listen to only a couple of simple instructions was an evolution.

Negative self-chatter during races is common, and it even creeps into the minds of elite athletes when they feel like they can't live up to internal or external expectations or pressures. Sometimes that causes them to formulate excuses in the middle of races. It can be devastating. And that's one of the reasons I preferred to exude only positive energy to my team.

Kuntz was 12th at state as a junior and came into the state meet a year later projected to finish about third. But he won it. I've often thought about what it was that made Greg a state champion. Here was a guy who could tie himself into knots mentally and get eighth at an invitational and then one month later run with complete control and win the state title.

It took a lot of positive reinforcement to get Kuntz to believe in himself. He put way too much pressure on himself. So we talked about it. I told him to keep busy before the big race. Block out the competition. That's a skill that's easier said than done on race day. It took rehearsing and reminding. He needed to stay distracted with something else, whether it was homework, reading, playing cards, or whatever.

Preparing Runners

Race "strategy" means paying attention to the details that go into being prepared. Figure 9.1 is a short checklist of things you might want to use to remind your runners before a big race. Some of them are tips for the

Figure 9.1   Prerace Checklist for Runners

☐ Make sure your shoes are double knotted.

☐ If you have a choice of where to stand on the starting line and the first turn on the course is a left, start on the right side of the starting line. And vice versa. You don't want to get boxed in right away.

☐ Don't always follow the crowd. Follow the course. Run the shortest distance possible.

☐ Be cool. Stay relaxed.

CONNOR! →☐ Don't lead unless you know you are going to win. Why would you want to be a rabbit for someone else?

☐ Run your race, not someone else's race.

☐ Your arms are your engine. Make sure they are active.

☐ If you're going up a hill, put your nose ahead of your toes.

☐ Pace the hill. Don't kill the hill.

☐ When you're going down a hill, don't flap your arms. It just slows you down.

☐ Run up a hill on your toes and down a hill on your heels.

→ ☐ When you start to feel depleted, think of a recent workout that you conquered and how good it felt when you finished it.

☐ Keep your eyes wide and alert. If your face is tight, you will run tight.

starting line of a big race. Others are merely common sense, which occasionally flies out the window when adrenaline and anxiety are running high.

Running Together

It would be great if each member of your top seven could run as fast as your No. 1. But that's seldom the case. Gaps open up between teammates during a race, and sometimes there's nothing you, as a coach, can do about them. So telling your team to run together doesn't always make sense.

Once you get a feel for your talent, discuss strategies. Maybe your third and fourth guys are similar and run nearly identical workouts. It makes sense then to suggest that they work together during the race. Running with a teammate in a race can help an athlete dig a little deeper, show a little more courage, and remain motivated.

The first one-third of a race usually takes care of itself. The runners come off the starting line charged up with adrenaline, and for the first five or six minutes they are usually sorting themselves out and establishing position. Fatigue normally doesn't begin to creep in until the second third, and that's a point in the race where it could be helpful to have a teammate nearby.

If your athletes are front-runners, they just want to get out and knock it down. They already expect to be up near the front and don't need the encouragement of seeing their teammates. They have the other runners in the lead pack to spur them on.

Regardless of the talent level, every runner on the starting line should begin the race with a positive attitude and feel invigorated by the opportunity to succeed. A new personal record and a chance to help the team effort, these two goals are universal in cross country.

Running in a Pack

It is easier to move in a pack of other runners than to run alone in the middle of a race. Whether it's near the lead or farther back, runners usually clump together over the course of a 5,000-meter race. Each pack creates its own minicompetition with runners trying to outduel opponents of similar pace and skill level. There is comfort in a pack. It's possible to draft behind someone and not catch all of the wind on a blustery day. And running in a group keeps the mind active and thinking because a wrong step or trip could spell disaster.

Runners should avoid getting stuck in the middle of a pack. When runners are boxed, they are forced into a moving space without the freedom to make choices about surging or passing. The better spot is at the back of a pack or on the side of it, where there is room to work and a way to keep moving forward. Ideally, your runners will remain vested in moving up, from one pack to the next, and try to finish as high as possible.

Moves between packs should be decisive. Getting stuck in no-man's-land is a surefire way to lose momentum, energy, and focus. Confidence is a big factor here. If runners know they can bridge the gap to the next group, they should make it happen. If they're not ready, it's OK to wait until the time feels right.

Knowing What to Expect

I usually found time on the Monday before a Wednesday dual meet to sit down and lay the meet out based on best guesses. Within a league format, most coaches know who the opponents are and have access to previous results. It usually isn't too difficult to figure out how a race might play out. Accuracy doesn't matter here, instead, the aim is a quick study to figure out whether the outcome will be one sided or whether it will be close. When you have it on paper, you can begin to see what it looks like and what factors might tip the scale in your favor.

Courtesy of Price Photography

Racing requires individual effort, but an athlete can feel lifted by the support of teammates while running in a pack.

At Mead, we were fortunate to develop a mystique around the program. Every school in the Greater Spokane League knew we were the nine-time state champions. And because of that, the other teams watched and scrutinized us. We knew we had the bull's-eye on our backs. But I spun that a different way. I told them, "You're wearing a jersey with so much power and energy, it's magical. We have a tradition, so let's keep it up. That jersey is worth a 10-meter lead before the race has even started." Now, I wouldn't go saying things like that in mixed company. But when I said it to my guys, they ate it up.

Before the meet, I usually tried to plant a few buzzwords. Matt Davis came up with a phrase that we liked: "Light as a feather, strong as a bear, and fast as a cheetah." When your middle-of-the-pack or end-of-the-pack runners take off from the starting line with those words on the brain, all it can do is help. The middle part of a race is where some people fall asleep and lose focus. This is the "take charge" phase, and it's where the runner wants to stay positive and begin to say those words. They can become a mantra until it's time to kick.

When the Going Gets Tough

Sometimes, in the midst of a race, a runner just knows it isn't his or her day. There are times when running is just painful for any number of reasons. In those moments, the runner has to find a way to survive. You don't want kids to throw in the towel and stop. In the long run, that will only make them feel worse. Even at the end of a long, tough race, there are rewards and satisfaction in finishing it.

When you see a kid who is struggling in a race, and you are certain that no injury is involved, there is little you can do as a coach but hope for the best and offer a few words of encouragement. Even very good runners have bad days and falter. But it's not life or death. I might shout something like, "Don't be a Geo Metro! Be a Porsche! You're only five minutes away!" When a runner is in survival mode, you just want to help the athlete stay with it mentally.

Getting Up After a Fall

Falls happen in races, but the challenge is to keep them from being so disruptive that your athlete can't recover. Morgan Uceny of the United States suffered a heartbreaking fall on the final lap of the women's 1,500-meter final at the 2012 Olympics. And she had fallen a year earlier in eerily similar fashion at the World Championships. Those falls were devastating because Uceny couldn't overcome them.

In cross country, a fall is most likely to happen near the start of the race, when a lot of bodies are pressed into a small space and a runner can get tangled up, tripped, or shoved to the ground. But in a 5,000-meter race, this shouldn't be a killer. There is lots of time to get back, get going, and remain patient. All is not lost. Falls also happen, sometimes, on down slopes when the weather is bad and footing is slippery. Again, these falls usually aren't game changers. At the Washington state championships back in 1968, a runner from Ferris High named Randy James fell coming off the starting line and then got up and won the race by 36 seconds.

At Mead, we rehearsed those sorts of setbacks. We practiced how to fall and avoid getting hurt, how to get back up, how to get our head back in the game, and how to press on with the goals of the race still intact. That way, when a fall happens, nobody freaks out.

Flying Elbows

Especially at the start of races, where kids are flying off the starting line and making sure that they have space, elbows can start flying. Your athletes might take an elbow to the chest that stuns them momentarily. Elbow or forearm contact could also send a runner to the ground. On this subject, I simply advise athletes to run competitively. Elbows will be thrown, and rarely is there ill-tempered intent behind them. Cross country runners, by and large, aren't that mean. It is part of the sport, so runners have to protect themselves and hold their ground.

Most people looked at the Mead teams and saw us as a polite group. I worked to make sure that was the case. I don't like cocky attitudes. I wanted to win with class. If another team seemed intent on trying to bully us or get under our skin, I'd tell my guys, "Beat them with your legs, not your arms or fists." There is never a reason for runners to shoot their mouths off.

Understanding the Limits of Control

So much of what happens in a cross country race is left to chance. For those 15 to 20 minutes, there is little a coach can do to affect the outcome. There are no time-outs. There are no second chances.

There are factors that come into play that you simply can't control. Your top athlete could suffer a season-ending injury, or your entire top five could graduate all at the same time and leave the cupboard bare. At Mead, I focused on keeping the mystique alive. I tried to get my runners to understand the power of the jersey, that the tradition woven into the fabric was something they could feed on and find some comfort in. I never wanted to add fuel to any doubts that the athletes might have. You'll be surprised sometimes by how far kids can go if you set them up to succeed.

For me, knowing what was controllable formed my race strategy.

- Encourage your athletes to maintain the pattern they have developed so that they are hydrated, nourished, and rested.
- Prevent mental lapses by reminding athletes to stay tuned in, alert, and frisky.
- If someone is having uncharacteristic problems in races, bonking, or otherwise running out of gas, address it. Have the runner touch base with a doctor and look into the possibilities of anemia or iron deficiency.

- Be prepared. Did you bring spikes the right length to fit the course conditions?
- Always arrive at the starting line 10 minutes before the scheduled race time, just in case something weird happens and the race goes off early.
- Keep an even keel. Even if your top runner is so nervous that he or she throws up in a trash can, there is never a reason for you, as a coach, to show concern or make a big deal out of it. Never panic. Never worry. Just say, "Isn't that great? He's doing what all the great ones do!"
- Coach your team based on the talent you have. It's nice for the top seven to finish within a minute of each other, but it's not always possible. Average teams can generally find a way to work together and feed off each other.
- Instill an attitude or establish the goal that no one on the team gets passed over the final 100 meters.
- Offer encouragement during a race that is helpful. Choose your words carefully. I sometimes yelled something at one of my runners like, "I need you to get five more!" Sometimes it was spontaneous, "You pass those five, and I'll get you a steak dinner!"
- Position yourself about 300 meters from the end of the race. When it's possible, you want to be able to salvage things at the end of the race with your cheering.
- Don't complicate the game.

Knowing what your team has been capable of in workouts is valuable information and should be a source of confidence. Every athlete on the team should be made aware of what their workouts mean when applied to the race. Even when something goes haywire, like a hailstorm or an untied shoelace, a well-prepared runner can absorb that situation on the fly, make necessary adjustments without panic or fear, and press on with the pace they know they can run. As a coach, it's important to continue to exude positivity while all of the scenarios, the controllable and uncontrollable, play out.

Changing Dynamics at Mead: 1997-2005

I was fortunate to guide my team to nine straight state championships, and that ride was a great thrill. But all good things come to an end. The Mead School District opened a second school, Mt. Spokane High School, which joined the Greater Spokane League in 1997. Suddenly, our school was split in two. Half of the kids who ordinarily would have come to Mead went to the new school, which started its own cross country program. We went from a three-year high school to a four-year.

Our program was strong enough to overcome that obstacle in the short term. But graduating six of our top seven from the 1996 team was an even bigger challenge. Additionally, a talented young runner named Tom Becker, who ran for us as a sophomore, went to Mt. Spokane because of how the neighborhood boundaries were drawn up. Our depth was diminished.

We put together a good season, but we simply weren't as good as University High, another member of the Greater Spokane League (GSL). U-High beat us 17-38 in a dual meet, our first loss in 10 years, ending a string of 79 GSL victories. U-High also beat us at Sunfair and then again at regionals. So it was no great surprise that University won the state title. We performed well to get second with 75 points.

My message was direct. I didn't want my guys to feel they'd let anyone down. I told the press, "This is the best Mead has competed (at state) in the last four years." We didn't throw in the towel. We just got beat by better runners. In fact, I thought we had probably overachieved. (Becker, by the way, won the first of his back-to-back state titles).

We had prepared for the end of the streak, knowing it was a probability. I had my team find the University kids after the state meet was over and shake their hands. I sought out Bob Barbero, the U-High coach, and personally congratulated him. It was the right thing to do.

In 1998 and 1999, University remained on top of the state. Mead was second and third at the state meet those two years. In 1999, we beat U-High in the dual meet 27-29 and won the regional but then had a bad day at state.

The final tally: University 81, Mt. Spokane 82, Mead 90. That one stung!

In 2000, brothers Chris and Jesse Fayant finished second and third, overall, to help us regain the state title. It happened again in 2001, with Jesse winning the individual title over favored Chris Lukezic and the team scoring 63 points, our lowest total since 1996. The rise of young stars Evan Garber and Laef Barnes helped us win it for the third year in a row in 2002.

In 2003, Garber won the individual title with a big effort to beat talented David Kinsella. Ferris, a GSL rival, won the team championship. The 2004 team placed second in the state meet but qualified to compete in the inaugural Nike Team Nationals (subsequently Nike Cross Nationals) under the name Tyson's Army and finished third in the first national championship for high school cross country.

Mead runners elected the club name Tyson's Army for their appearance at Nike Team Nationals.

In 2005, Ferris beat us again in a close competition for the state title. That came after an exciting win over Ferris in our dual meet earlier in the season. Again, we qualified for Nike Cross Nationals, and this time placed fourth with Taylor Nepon and Steven Gimpel leading the way.

In 2006, I took a college coaching job at the University of Kentucky. I returned to high school coaching briefly at South Eugene High School in Oregon and then was hired as the cross country and track coach at Gonzaga University in Spokane.

Summary

The best race strategy I know is to help your team understand that "the hay is in the barn." The sum of the workouts completed is the level you will be at on race day. Teach your athletes to come to the race prepared and confident, and the results will take care of themselves.

- The best advice I can give about race strategy is this: Keep it simple!

- It's OK to give your athletes a long leash. Don't hold them back. Let them explore their courage.

- At Mead, our prerace mantra was "Go out hard. Take charge. Have fun."

- Negative self-talk can be harmful. Emit positive energy and encourage prerace activities that keep the mind off the race if it is becoming burdensome.

- Running in packs comes with risks such as getting boxed in, but it also has rewards. It's better than being caught in no-man's-land.

- Plant a few buzzwords in your team's collective head before the race to get them fired up.

- Some days feel worse than others. When the race is going badly, help your athlete find a way to survive it.

- Falls and thrown elbows happen. Runners should respond quickly, forget it, and move on. Rehearse challenges so they don't cause panic.

- Come to meets prepared and focus on the things that you can control.

PART IV

COACHING FOR COMPETITIONS

CHAPTER 10 Preparing for Meets

In addition to coaching your team and training it to compete in dual meets, invitationals, and end-of-season championship meets, a time will usually come when you must host a meet. Particularly if you are at a school with a reasonably good home course, and you may even put on several meets a year or host an annual invitational. I preferred to take my team to meets and let someone else worry about the details of hosting, although we certainly held one or more meets each year at Mead.

Some coaches revel in hosting big events and are good at managing all of the details. Big invitational meets are usually annual events with long histories. The schools (and coaches) that operate those meets take on a litany of additional responsibilities to handle the management and operations of a large sporting event. Although this chapter focuses on the details of hosting a meet, it also reviews how to prepare for your meets on the road.

Rehearsing the Course

As stated previously, I was fortunate that the Spokane School District allowed us to travel by bus to a meet site two days in advance of the competition so that we could go over the courses before running on them. This privilege was accorded for Greater Spokane League meets, and we took full advantage.

Course rehearsal days were important. Not only did they give us a chance to study the terrain we would run on, but they also started the build-up and excitement for the race. We practiced starts and visualized success at the finish line, sometimes employing the sprint, float, sprint drill (see chapter 7).

Not every school has the luxury of course rehearsals. And certainly, when we traveled to invitational meets farther away on the weekends, we had only a couple of hours before the race to get acquainted with the course. But I strongly recommend taking advantage of any opportunity to familiarize your runners with the course. Also, discuss potential locations for setting up your team's camp and know ahead of time where the bathrooms are and where the buses will be parked. When you can eliminate the guesswork and unknowns ahead of time, race day becomes a lot less stressful.

Hosting a Meet

It is a point of pride to be able to entertain other programs for a cross country meet. It's a chance to show your respect for other teams and coaches, and it's an opportunity to put your best foot forward as a host. Every member of your team should be well-versed in the responsibility that comes with being a

Three Common Mistakes by Meet Hosts

Not all meets are created equal when it comes to organization and a well-planned layout. Even good meets run into problems from time to time, but they are correctable.

The first common problem is a bottleneck at the finish line. Traffic at the finish can also be dangerous when athletes who have sprinted toward the line need space beyond it to slow down and the athletes who have already finished are filling some of that space.

A long finish chute alleviates a lot of problems. Finish volunteers and spotters can help move finished runners forward into the chutes and clear out space at the line. Second and third chutes can be used if there is not enough room to construct one long chute. This requires having enough volunteers to jump in and open a second chute when the first one fills up. The chutes are parallel and can be opened and closed with finish line flagging.

A second issue is keeping athletes in the correct order at the finish line. Chip timing automatically solves this problem, but without it, one or two people must be on hand to sort out the finish order. Better yet, have two timing systems going at once in case one goes down or has a problem. The standard procedure is to have videotaping of the finish so that it can be reviewed if there is a question over finish order or time. The highest priority should be on correct place, and correct finish time second. Of course, ideally you want accuracy in both. (Double and triple check the results before announcing them).

Finally, you never want to be caught as a meet host with inadequate medical resources. Be sure to have trainers nearby. Have ice. And make sure someone has access to a cell phone in case a 911 call needs to be made. (This is almost never a problem nowadays).

gracious host. Hospitality should rule the day while opposing teams are on your campus.

Here are the items that go into hosting a meet:

- **Find a meet manager.** This might be you, but you can also find someone who is qualified and delegate that role. The meet manager is in charge of running the meet and making sure all of the details of the event are executed. This person has to be organized and plugged into every aspect of the meet including officiating, timing, communicating with visiting teams, and promoting the meet. The meet manager assigns all of the tasks related to hosting the meet. Coaches, volunteers, parents, the athletic director, and teachers should attend a preseason meeting in which the meet manager lays out everyone's responsibilities. (Order pizza for the whole group to make sure everyone shows up!)

- **Accurately lay out the course.** It may not be exactly 5,000 meters, but it needs to match the course maps that you will hand out. Ideally, you want a wide-open starting area with wide starting lanes for each team. A perfect start allows 200 to 400 meters before the first turn. This is especially true for big invitationals in which hundreds of runners are on the course at the same time. Use red flagging for right turns and blue flagging for left turns. (A yellow flag indicates the course goes straight ahead, which may be helpful where trails intersect). Err on the side of overmarking the course. The course should end with a nice straightaway of at least 100 meters. A two- or three-loop course is friendly for spectators. It is nice to have a finish area close to the start area (for the sake of timing, positioning officials, and retrieving warm-up clothes).

- **Invite coaches to bring their teams for a course rehearsal.** This requires having maps ready and the course lined one or two days before the meet.

- **Provide each coach a map.** Include mile marks, the start and finish, and course directions that are easy to understand and follow (see figure 10.1).

- **Place cones, markers, and posts.** Mark the route at appropriate spots to indicate corners and turns. Be sure that these indicators are easy to follow. The

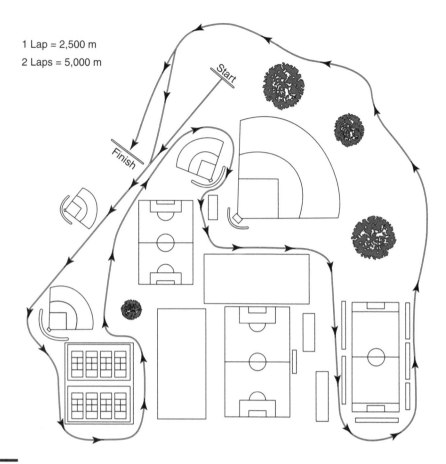

1 Lap = 2,500 m
2 Laps = 5,000 m

Start

Finish

FIGURE 10.1 Course map.

last thing you want is for a runner to make a mistake and head the wrong way or get lost. I used a post with a number on a paper plate as mile markers.

- **Line the course with chalk.** Better yet, chalk both sides of the lane width as prescribed in the handbook for the National Federation of State High School Associations. (The course must be at least three feet wide (1 m) at its narrowest point).

- **Use orange field paint or small flags.** Use these to mark sprinkler heads or other potential hazards.

- **Place volunteers at points that require direction.** Volunteers should be stationed by driveways, or at high-traffic areas that could cause confusion.

- **Locate a portable clock near the finish line.** This way athletes and spectators can see finish times.

- **Make a cool finish line.** Whether that involves an arch of balloons is up to you, but make sure it is easily visible and functional. Make sure the chutes are long, and use lots of flagging for crowd control.

- **Choose an appropriate option for timing.** For a dual meet, you might be able to handle the timing with a couple of volunteers and a handheld timer. (That requires two people). For larger meets, the norm is a computerized timing device that includes a finish camera. Also for bigger meets, with six or more teams, you'll need to hire a professional timing company. Entry fees usually cover the cost of the finish-line crew. For a larger meet, use chip timing if it's affordable. The price has come down considerably with the advent of disposable chips on the race bib.

- **Provide numbered bibs for large meets or tags for dual meets.** For dual meets, provide tags that can be easily gathered at the finish line and put on a clipboard. This old-school method is still used in Spokane. Simply print address labels listing the athlete's name, school, and year in school. For bigger meets, you'll need bibs with numbers.

- **Have a copy of the most recent high school federation handbook.** It is best to have this onsite in case there is a need to refer to the rules or to give direction on language, uniforms, jewelry, and so on.

- **Provide course marshals.** It's nice to have experienced marshals on the course, but it's usually not necessary for a smaller meet.

- **Have an experienced starter in place.** Over time, a coach creates a network of local starters, judges, and finish-line gurus. A judge is important because he or she will make the final decision on close races if there are no cameras. If a camera is in place, the judge is the official who will review the photo. Clerking officials review athletes at the starting area for proper uniforms and enforce rules on jewelry. (In the United States, watches are legal but bracelets, necklaces, and rings are not). Judges also make calls on missed turns and rule on poor sportsmanship or other behavior that might lead to disqualifications.

- **Place a couple of tables near the finish line.** These are for printed results, garbage bags, water, and so on.

- **Assign someone to make announcements over a loudspeaker, if possible.** They should start alerting runners 10 minutes before the race to make their way to the starting line. That gives officials time to check for proper racing attire and go over the start commands.

- **Recruit a minimum of 10 volunteers.** Even for a dual meet, figure on five for the finish line, a couple at the starting line, and someone at key corners. Try to find someone other than parents to fill these roles. Parents want to watch their kids. Staff members, alumni, or injured athletes can handle these jobs.

- **Have someone lead the runners if your course is particularly tough.** Consider using a small tractor, like a John Deere Gator, or someone on a bicycle. Perhaps more important, is having a sweeper trail the race in case a runner gets hurt.

- **Order portable toilets if you need to.** Access to schools and park facilities may not be adequate. Additionally, make sure you are stocked with toilet paper.

- **Provide access for spectators with disabilities or who use wheelchairs.** This is especially important for parking and places to safely watch the race.

- **Provide space for your team to have a "fort" with a team tent and gathering area.** Make sure there is also room for the other schools to set up their forts as well.

- **Know in advance where the buses will park and understand that system.** It might be wise to put a volunteer in charge of parking, including buses.

- **Assign a group to clean up all litter after the meet.** The clean-up crew will also take down the course flags and cones, and lock up the facilities that need to be secured.

- **Use snow fencing to create a barrier if there is an admission fee.** Set it up to create the inside (course and spectator areas) and outside. Some schools use invitational meets as fund-raisers.

- **Order awards.** High school athletes love awards, whether medals, T-shirts, trophies, or whatever you have to give them. It is common at big invitationals to offer awards to the top teams and individuals. Do not to wait until the

Figure 10.2   Away Meet Checklist

☐ Make an itinerary for the meet, which includes the bus schedule. (You can do this months in advance.)

☐ Call the bus barn the day before the meet to verify that the bus is coming.

☐ About a week before the meet, prepare an early dismissal list for all teachers.

☐ Request a bulletin announcement to advertise the competition if at home (two or three days in advance).

☐ Have the following on hand:

- Water jugs
- Cups
- Ice
- Medical kit
- Extra jersey and shorts (or two)
- Variety of spikes, plus spike wrench and vise-grips
- Emergency phone list
- Timer or watch
- Clipboard

- Several pencils
- Team tent, plus three or four large blue tarps
- Camera or someone in place to take photos
- Several towels
- Rain gear for coaches and extras for runners (try to keep the bus on site when the weather is bad).
- Roll of toilet paper

☐ Make sure someone is in charge of snacks (e.g., bread, bananas, peanut butter, jelly).

☐ Warn athletes to secure and monitor their gear so that it isn't stolen, particularly their cell phones.

☐ Use garbage bags with kids' names on them to stow warm-up gear at the starting line.

☐ Remind athletes to take off jewelry and store it if they forgot to leave it at home.

---

last minute to plan the awards. Order them as soon as you know how many you need so that you have time to fix mistakes (e.g., misspellings, wrong numbers) if you have to.

- **Sell T-shirts.** This is a potential revenue source if you are trying to use the meet as a fund-raiser. A well-designed meet shirt is a keepsake with the name of the meet and the year. They are consistently strong sellers.

Whether the meet is home or away, there are items you want to have handy and chores that need to be carried out or assigned. And there are also a few other things to think about. Figure 10.2 is an away race-day to-do list.

Scoring in Cross Country

Scoring in cross country is pretty simple. Here is an overview of the basics.

- Lowest score wins.
- The first five (out of seven team members who participate) count for scoring. Their finish places are added together and compared to the totals of the opposing teams.

- A perfect score is 15 points, the result of sweeping the top five places. A perfect dual meet result is 15 to 50. That is the result of the winning team taking the top seven places and the losing team's scorers finishing 8th through 12th. Take note that the winning team's sixth and seventh runners did not count in the score, but they did displace their opponent's placers by occupying those two positions. Every runner and every place matters.

- A tie in the team score is broken by the finish places of the sixth runners on each team.

Following are three scenarios that can be used to further understand the concepts of team scoring in cross country:

Example 1

Team A places 1st, 2nd, 3rd, 9th, and 10th for a total of 25 points.

Team B places 4th, 5th, 6th, 7th, and 8th for a total of 30 points.

Note: If a team goes 1-2-3 at a dual, it wins no matter what. To win, a team must either break up an opponent's top three or try to sweep the top three spots.

Example 2

Team A places 1st, 3rd, 5th, 7th, and 9th for 25 points.

Team B places 2nd, 4th, 6th, 8th, and 10th for 30 points.

Note: An alternating order of finish results in a win for the team with the individual winner. The lesson here is to try to run as a pack. Bunch to win!

Example 3

Team A places 1st, 2nd, 4th, 11th, and 12th and scores 30 points.

Team B places 3rd, 5th, 6th, 7th, 8th, (9th), and (10th) and scores 29 points.

Note: Look how important the sixth and seventh finishers are here. They push back the opponent. In this case, team B wins because its seventh finisher beat the team A's fourth runner. If team B's seventh finisher had finished 11th, the score would have been a tie, and thus the sixth runners on each team would have decided the outcome of the meet. So remember, every member of the team is vital to the team's success. Every place is crucial. I told my runners, "Never let someone pass you at the end of the race or in the finish chute because you can never know if the outcome of the entire meet is riding on you."

Developing an Itinerary

Whenever your team travels, lay out a thoughtful, organized itinerary so that everyone in the party stays on the same page. I printed them off and made sure each person on the trip had a copy and made them as detailed as possible. This goes for dual meets across town and plane trips. See figure 10.3 for an example of an itinerary printout that I gave to the team and parents before leaving for the Stanford Invitational.

Figure 10.3 Sample Away Meet Itinerary

STANFORD INVITATIONAL

Friday, Sept. 26

9:15 a.m.	Arrive at Horizon Airlines check-in
10:30 a.m.	Depart flight #2327 for Seattle
12:28 p.m.	Depart Alaska #380 for San Jose
2:33 p.m.	Arrive in San Jose
3:30 p.m.	Check in: Sheraton Palo Alto
4 p.m.	30-min. jog + 12 $\times$ grass strides @ Stanford
5:30 p.m.	Dinner @ Olive Garden
10 p.m.	Lights out

Saturday, Sept. 27

9 a.m.	Breakfast JV
11 a.m.	Breakfast varsity
1:30 p.m.	JV race
3:05 p.m.	Varsity race
3:35 p.m.	College races
6 p.m.	Take in San Francisco
11 p.m.	Lights out

Sunday, Sept. 28

7:30 a.m.	One-hour run on Stanford area trails
9:30 a.m.	Swim, clean up, breakfast
10:45 a.m.	Arrive at San Jose Airport
12:09 p.m.	Depart Alaska #327 for Seattle
3 p.m.	Depart Horizon #2346 for Spokane

Costs

1. Transportation: Provided by Mead School District

2. Food: I'd recommend bringing $35. Our primary meal is around $12 at Olive Garden. Other meals will be budget prices plus grocery store stuff.

3. Lodging is provided FREE thanks to a wonderful Mead Cross Country supporter!

4. Do you want to buy some Stanford stuff? Meet Ts are about $15.

NO SPIKES ON STANFORD COURSE! WEAR WAFFLE FLATS!

Summary

Preparing for meets means doing all of the things that will take you to the starting line with nothing to worry about except running the race. Cross country is a simple sport, but it is supported by myriad details that must be addressed.

- For most coaches, hosting meets is part of the job description. Some coaches put a lot of energy into a large annual meet. More than likely, you will be obligated to host a meet, whether a dual or something larger.

- Course rehearsals are a great way to prepare for a meet. They allow your runners to get familiar with the course and with the idea of closing hard at the finish.

- Whether hosting a meet or traveling to one, be prepared and organized well in advance.

- A carefully planned itinerary is essential for all meets, but it is particularly important for trips with elaborate travel details.

CHAPTER 11

Coaching Meets

Arriving on game day with the positive attitude that the hay is already in the barn is a critical component to being confident and ready to go. At meets, it is a coach's responsibility to make sure the team arrives early enough to set up the team fort. In this chapter, I walk through a premeet speech and a postmeet talk, and I outline the roles for each athlete, parent, and coach. I told my guys that workouts were work, and that races were play. So cross country is the "game" that we're playing.

I never cared much about keeping splits during cross country meets. I might carry a clipboard and chart the team score, but usually I gave myself the job of taking photos. The other assistants had designated spots on the course where they'd shout encouragement. My assistants did more of the cheering than I did. I was busy taking photos, and I have them from every meet during my years at Mead.

Prerace Speeches

Running while fueled by inspiration is great, but it can also be overdone. I never wanted my guys to get too hyper before a meet because they started to lose the necessary calmness and ability to conserve energy in the hours before a meet. Mostly, I just wanted the guys to feel free and loose, confident, and enthusiastic.

My preference was to have a talk three or four days before a big meet such as the state cross country championships so the team didn't get too worked up. That doesn't mean I didn't pull out a letter from a past champion and read it to the guys. I would ask legends of the past to write letters to the future team so that I could keep our past alive in the program. Hearing from a former teammate who had been where they were and succeeded built a sense of being connected to greatness. When I read the letters to the team, they looked up to and felt connected to these legends, such as Chris Lewis, Matt and Micah Davis, and Evan Garber. But I think it's important to remain loose and relaxed rather than intense and fired up.

Sometimes, I would take the team to the auditorium at the school, turn the lights down, and play "We Are the Champions" by Queen. I'd tell the guys to listen to the lyrics, visualize the warm-up, visualize the race, and feel so excited that there's no doubt about giving

A Letter From Evan Garber to Mead Cross Country Runners

This is a prestate letter from Evan Garber, who was the Washington Class 4A cross country champion in 2003.

To the MEN OF MEAD:

Last week you ran to qualify (for state) and almost won. Now you will run to win. It will not be easy. You must be prepared to suffer. You must have the attitude that you can take any amount of punishment in order to win. "You are gonna eat lightning and crap thunder." For those very few moments of pain you will remember for a lifetime how you overcame the odds and became state champions. You will be state champions for the rest of your lives and that is a very special thing. You have the best coaches and are the best-prepared team. No one peaks for the state meet like Mead does. The race will be close. Every place will count. The team that is willing to suffer the most will win. The team that is the most competitive and most unwilling to give up will win. Every one of you is capable of great things. I know that Laef Barnes is the best runner in the state of Washington right now. It doesn't matter what has happened so far this year. You are capable of being the individual state champion. I have seen you run some amazing races off of pure guts and that is what you need to do today, put everything on the line and just let loose. I remember Jesse Fayant was not the favorite to win, but at the state meet his senior year, he beat one of the fastest milers in the country by outkicking him. He outkicked a guy who said that if he could see the finish line then he could not be outkicked. Jesse believed that he was going to win and he didn't let anything stop him.

Last year I got second at regionals, but I didn't care because all that mattered was how well I performed at state. In the final 500 meters of the race at state, David Kinsella had taken off and it looked like he was going to win. It looked as if I was going to get third place and I had almost accepted it. I was in pain. I was suffering and could have so easily given up. But I was not willing to give up! I said to myself: "Go after him. You can still get him." I was so determined to win that I forgot how much pain I was in, and I dug deep. I gave it everything I had. I kept saying to myself: "I'm gonna win. I'm gonna win!" I found another gear and in the last 20 meters I blew by David Kinsella and won the state title. That is what you need to do in order to be state champions. You need to put yourself through pain and stay positive. Be competitive, and don't let yourself give up. Run for your team, and run with guts. I will leave you with something Matt Davis wrote to the team my freshman year. It is something that I like to repeat in my head when negative thoughts pop up:

Light as a feather
Strong as a bear
Fast as a cheetah

Best of skill,
Evan Garber

---

their best. I'd tell them, "You're going to give that jersey a ride like it's never had before." Or I might use something from the Prefontaine movie soundtrack or a song by U2. But again, I advise doing this a few days before the big meet and not the night before.

About two minutes before the race started, I typically gathered the team for a huddle near the start line. And the message was always simple.

Go out. Take charge. Have fun.

Feed off each other. Have a blast.

Nobody passes you in the last mile.

Go fishing! See how many you can reel in.

Low score wins. Go get 'em!

These are short phrases that the athletes may be able to remember once the starter's gun goes off and the adrenaline kicks in and all of the bodies fly into motion.

A prerace cheer is a fun way to let off some bottled-up emotion prior to taking a position on the starting line.

The kids got into the habit of doing a cheer by themselves as I moved away to find my spot on the course. It was an old Welsh rugby chant that I learned from a guy I met in the 1970s. I introduced it at Shorecrest before it became a fixture at Mead.

"Uggy-uggy-uggy!" shouts one part of the group.

"Ugg! Ugg! Ugg!" responds the other.

It's light-hearted, meaningless, and serves only one purpose: Firing up and getting ready to pounce off the starting line.

Some coaches run from one end of the course to the other, burning off their anxiety and coaching runners at every possible moment. I felt that sort of thing was unnecessary. Sure, I and the assistant coaches—plus teammates and parents—find spots from which to cheer. But I almost didn't care about the split times the kids were running, I didn't feel compelled to watch the start of the race, and I almost never ran or appeared overly excited during a race.

Typically, I had my camera with me and was steady enough to take photos. That distraction might have been a good thing because it gave me something to do. I trusted that my athletes would take care of themselves, and that's the best feeling a coach can have while a race is in progress. If the kids are too dependent on the coach—and a coach can't be in all places at once—it's a sign that they're not prepared to be on their own. You run the risk that the athletes will have stage fright.

After I delivered a few words, I said good-bye and walked away 600 to 700 meters. I sometimes took a peek at the start and then maneuvered to a place where I maybe had a chance to say something to them. I liked to be 300 to 500 meters from the finish line in case a final instruction was necessary, something like, "We need your help! Dig deeper! Get two more; get two more!"

I was never too invested in the score while the race as going on. I maybe said to our guys, "We're behind by two points," even if I had no idea what the score was. Typically, one of the assistants kept tabs on the score so that we had at least some idea how it would turn out at the end. But I didn't mind the wait for the announcement to be official. I liked the anticipation and build-up of the moment right before the winner was announced.

Sometimes I'd take the kids aside and say, "I don't know, guys. It's awful close." It built suspense. More often than not, though, at Mead, there was very little suspense. When the top three are wearing your jersey, or six of the top seven, everyone knows how it turned out.

The prerace talk is little more than a quick chance to offer a final thought and calm nerves. As a coach, you need to emanate confidence in the moments before a race. Your runners should feed off your demeanor—cool, calm, and excited to go.

Postrace Talk

After the cool-down, I brought the team together to sit down so I could say something positive about what had happened. In 1997,

when our dual meet win streak of 10 years was ended by University, I had a speech already prepared.

I didn't dwell on anything negative in the wake of a race. If a kid felt like the race didn't go well, I told him it's OK to feel bad for five minutes, but then smile. I might have pointed out a few things that needed to be worked on over the coming week. Sometimes it was something as simple as suggesting we do a little less because guys appeared tired. Or it might have been to suggest a confidence-builder workout to remind them they were fit. Sometimes I suggested we go on a "vision quest" run on the trails just to get refreshed again. Focus on the positive. The postrace talk is always a glass-half-full meeting. It's a time for doling out praise.

I also had each assistant coach say something to the group, pointing out something that went well that day. And also, the team captains had a turn to say what they felt. Sometimes we concluded with a big group hug and a Popsicle for everyone.

At the end of the state meet, the postrace talk was even simpler. If we won it, the

In the aftermath of a race, always accentuate the positive and give praise. Nip any negativity in the bud and deal with any problems over the coming week.

coaches were launched into the nearest pond. Then we headed back to the hotel (we always had late checkout), got into the hot tub, celebrated, went out for pizza, and let the kids scream and be happy.

Postrace Work

Occasionally, you might be involved in a low-key meet that feels like little more than a glorified workout. And in those cases, you might decide that there is value in doing a little more when the race is over. If a meet hasn't been too strenuous, and the athletes are prepared for it, you might have them jog home four or five miles (6.4-8 km). Or maybe they could gather after the meet is over for 12 grass strides. Sometimes it's good to do a little bit more work, to show your athletes that every day is geared toward the overall goal of peaking for the state meet—and that certain low-pressure meets are merely speed bumps along the way.

Summary

Coaching meets can be delicate because emotions run high and everyone on the team is pulling toward a successful outcome. Do what you can to keep it simple by giving only a few instructions and by exuding confidence.

- On race day, it's the coach's job to be prepared and inspire confidence. Part of that means showing that you have confidence in your runners and allowing them to trust their training.
- The mission of a prerace talk should be to calm nerves.
- Try to give athletes no more than one or two things to think about while they are racing.
- The postrace talk is a time to dole out praise, not to be critical.
- On occasion, if the race wasn't stressful or taxing, an extra workout might make good sense.

PART V

COACHING EVALUATION

CHAPTER 12 | Evaluating Runners' Performance

Every cross country race during the regular season is a midterm exam that leads to the final (districts, regionals, or state). Just as a spelling test gauges the ability to formulate letters into words, a cross country race is an indicator of fitness, toughness, courage, and of teamwork. Although the results of the meet don't always tell the complete story of how a race unfolded, it is impossible to get away from the bottom line. Twenty-third place, for instance, is twenty-third place no matter how you slice it. A personal record is the definitive achievement in the athletic career of a high school cross country runner. Once you've broken 16:00 for 5,000 meters, that fact can never be taken away from you. Meet results are the primary way to evaluate a runner's performance, and it is the obligation of every high school coach to study them at the conclusion of the meet.

Analyzing the Stats

After every meet, I went home and typed up the results of each race and made photo copies early the next morning (see figure 12.1). Every kid on the team got a copy of the results, which included comments specific to each of them. Plus, I wrote an overall message

about how Mead fared and what it all meant going forward. Today, it might not be necessary to print out pages. You might send out a group e-mail instead.

Extensive record keeping is necessary in cross country. Every coach should keep multiple copies of every meet's results and have quick access to them for the sake of reference. It is important to be able to chart the progress of runners during the course of a single season or over the course of four years.

For every meet—dual, invitational, or championship—I included some kind of inspirational message about how each runner fared. I might have noted an improvement or a new PR. I checked against carefully researched top-10 lists for each course in the city—a freshman list, sophomore list, junior list, and senior list—and took special care to note new entries.

Kids love data, and cross country is full of it. I encourage any coach to be aware of course records, top-10 lists, personal bests, the gaps between runners one through seven, and any other data you might find pertinent.

After figuring out the relevance of the data and taking the opportunity to acknowledge every runner's effort, you can crunch those numbers again. Use the most recent race

Figure 12.1 Postmeet Evaluation Sheet

GREATER SPOKANE DUAL COMPETITION

University High School's Home Course, Liberty Lake

As the headlines said in this morning's *Spokesman-Review:* Panthers serve notice. "The hunter has become the hunted, thanks in part to Mead sophomore Jesse Fayant, who was part of a gritty four-runner effort. In a season-opening Greater Spokane League cross country meet befitting the state's top three teams, Fayant's sprint to third place helped the Panthers to a 27-29 victory over the defending champion and top-rated University Titans. Caught in the crossfire was Mt. Spokane, which lost 27-29 to the Titans and 22-33 to Mead."*

What great stuff guys! Note feedback:

Chris Fayant (15:51) 2nd Place. Only 6 seconds off winning! Nice effort for the team. You gave University's No. 1 runner, Max Schmidt, (15:45) all he could handle on his tough home course. I know you are on fire, Chris!

Jesse Fayant (16:10) 3rd Place. You edged the No. 2 University runner, Brandon Stum, in a same-time photo finish! Just think, Jesse, if you get beat, our team gets beat with a reverse score. You ran incredibly tough on the second hill, and you really were brave coming up that last 40-meter hill to the finish chute. Nice job. Some day you will be a state champion. You are only a sophomore.

Kelly Compogno (16:24) 5th place. You beat University's No. 3 runner by 28 seconds! Great pacing and focus. You told me you were going to have no mental lapses during the run. It was evident that you didn't.

Nate Boyer (16:40) 6th place. You ran like a veteran over this tough three-mile (1.5 × 2 loops) Liberty Lake course! Finishing 12 seconds ahead of University's No. 3 runner was huge. You showed the value of depth up front.

Patrick Chessar (17:09) 11th place. You are our No. 5 runner and thus count in our team score. You were only 17 seconds behind University's No. 3 runner, 13 seconds behind their No. 4, and 12 seconds behind their No. 5! We'll need you closer as the season progresses. You can run with Boyer. Pack up and feed off of him. You help Nate, and Nate helps you, and this helps the team. Keep believing.

Tim Schuermer (17:15) 12th place. You are our No. 6 runner. You ran really well for a young sophomore. You will get stronger. Don't be afraid to go out a bit harder with Nate Boyer. We need to pack up more. It will come. Nice closure over the last 400 meters!

Bryan Becherini (17:16) 13th place. You beat University's no. 7 runner by 25 seconds and were running in a nice pack with your buddies Schuermer and Chessar. You, too, are only a sophomore. I am excited to see how you progress throughout the season. Keep believing and knowing you will help our team shock people like we did today!

*Mike Vlahovich. September 23, 1999. "Panthers Serve Notice." *Spokesman Review.*

---

results to realign goal paces and establish new date paces. For example, if an athlete had a preseason goal of running 16:00 for 5,000 meters (77-second pace per 400 meters) and achieved that in the middle of the season, it would be time to come up with a new goal. A reasonable adjustment would be a goal of 15:40, which would be 5:02-mile pace or 75-second 400 meters pace. That athlete would have a date pace of 77 seconds and would aim for 75 seconds when doing goal-paced intervals. For rapidly improving athletes, these adjustments could become an ongoing process. And it's exciting when young runners are exploring their potential and finding that they have more that they can give.

Another way to evaluate results is to examine the amount of time between your No. 1 runner and your No. 7. This is the spread. A top seven that finishes within 60 seconds of one another creates an A group for training. Many of them may even share the same date pace and goal pace, which is beneficial because they can go through the same workout together. They can feed off each other.

As an example, you might have a workout that is seven × 1,000 meters, and the date pace is 16:00, so each interval would be done at 3:12. Or you could alternate them with goal pace (3:08 per 1,000 equates to a 15:40 target). Each member of the top seven could lead an interval, beginning with the seventh man and finishing with the first. This sort of workout creates a great team feeling and also teaches pace.

If one or more runner in the group is running out of gas—either in the last mile of a race or in workouts—you can adjust the workout. You might start the workout with four or five 1,000-meter intervals at date pace, then go up to goal pace for the sixth, and ask the runners to dig deep for the last 1,000 (sub-3:00). The recovery time is up to you, usually five to six minutes for each interval. Always make sure athletes get a full recovery.

Error on the side of more recovery than less. As you gain experience, you will begin to gauge appropriate recovery from body language, but heart rate is a good indicator as well. One thing that I recommend athletes keep in their journal is their resting heart beat. They should check it every morning when they wake up. If it is abnormally high (like 10 beats or more above normal) it could be a sign of not enough recovery. Resting heart beats vary. Many top runners have a resting heart rate of about 50 beats per second. (Steve Prefontaine's was about 40.) In the midst of interval training, recover with a light jog. When the heart rate is back to 90-110, it's generally safe to start the next interval.

Positive feedback at the conclusion of a race is an important part of race-day coaching.

Rewarding Accomplishments

Something else I loved to derive from meet results was awards. Runner of the Meet. Most Inspirational. Biggest PR.

I tried to make those awards mean something. It could be free pizza at the Monday Pizza gathering, or perhaps MVP privileges meant the first pick of seats on the bus the next time we went somewhere. I usually gave the MVP award to the runner who passed the most people in the last 400 meters of the race. I made a point of recognizing our sixth and seventh guys when they beat top-five guys from another team. I wanted the team to know they had made a difference.

Our PR Tradition

For a while, we had a tradition of making necklaces. Each new personal record was worth a new gold bead. A course record was worth another special bead. If a kid beat the No. 5 guy from another team, he got another bead. The necklaces grew over time, and became the symbols for meeting benchmarks and achieving goals.

Managing a Plateau

Continued progress is always the goal, but sometimes it doesn't come easily. A runner can get stuck in a pattern of producing the same performance meet after meet, or maybe even regress and lose a coveted top-seven spot on the team.

If a kid was discouraged that he had run 17:44, 17:41, and 17:43 in three consecutive meets, I told him not to worry. Runners and coaches must remember that every course is different. If a runner applies himself or herself in practice and completes the workouts on the schedule, eventually a breakthrough will come. This is where belief in the training and a positive attitude come into play.

What's toughest to deal with is the prospect of slipping out of the varsity top seven because performance is lagging or other runners are challenging the pecking order. If a runner in the top seven was in danger of falling out of the varsity group, I had a one-on-one meeting to discuss the situation. I offered positive feedback and told him to eat right, sleep right, and trust the training. If fatigue was the problem, I might have dialed back a workout or two or left him out of a competition so he got hungry again.

Shaking Up the Lineup

I didn't let one meet define who was in the varsity top seven. I preferred to stay loyal to the kid who had been part of the top seven all season and had shown consistency. Usually, this was someone that I had been able to rely on in the past.

If a member of the JV squad tears it up and scores a massive new PR—and runs faster than a top-seven runner—it's important to be upfront with the runners involved. To the JV runner, I offered my congratulations, maybe even told him he had become the No. 1 alternate, but I also informed him that he had to maintain that improved level in order to crack the varsity group. I bumped that kid into a faster workout group and let him begin to shadow excellence and see how he held up.

To the runner in danger of losing a top-seven spot, I made it clear that I still had faith in him, but that I would make the decision that was best for the team. That may be a bitter pill to swallow, but a team player understands what's most important: the team. Usually, a runner had to get sick or lose decisively in a head-to-head competition to lose a top-seven spot.

If the competition for the seventh spot continues to remain close, it's important to spell out the expectations to both runners in advance. A head-to-head race may tip the scales one way or the other, but ultimately the coach may have to make a tough decision. I recall two or three situations where it was a difficult call to make. Sometimes you have a guy coming on late in the season and you have to go with him because he's consistently nailing it down.

Courtesy of Price Photography

Encourage up-and-coming runners to challenge the top seven runners, but make consistency the marker for gaining a top seven spot.

From my own experience at the University of Oregon I know what it is like to be the eighth guy on the team as well as the seventh. Back then we ran a six-mile time trial. Whoever won it got to be seventh man.

In high school, it's a little brutal to put that much pressure on kids trying to sort who is No. 7 and who is No. 8. When it was a toss-up, I tended to stick with the kid who had previously been entrenched with the varsity group. There were other factors to consider. Who had demonstrated a superior work ethic? Who had performed better in practice? Who was more loyal to the goals of the team?

Summary

Race results are the ultimate evaluation of a runners' performance. Fitness, competitiveness, anxiety, and toughness all tend to be reflected in the finish time. Each race is a stepping-stone to the one that comes next, so keep thorough records to track every member of the team and parse the data in ways that inform upcoming workouts.

- Race results are the black-and-white evidence for evaluating your runners' fitness and performance.

- Keep extensive records to track the history of your team year after year. Carefully evaluate each meet's results and print copies for your athletes that include constructive comments and praise.

- Use meet data to adjust date pace and goal pace as your athletes make progress during the course of the season.

- Recognize individuals for their achievements through awards after races.

- The difference between being the No. 7 and No. 8 on a varsity cross country team is huge. When it's a close call, make sure expectations are spelled out and that the process is fair. Ultimately, it's your call.

CHAPTER 13 Evaluating Your Program

Start the assessment of any high school cross country team by asking basic questions about the integrity, sportsmanship, and study habits of the athletes involved. First and foremost, as a coach, you are teaching life skills and buttressing that with heavy doses of discipline and work ethic. Adopting a running lifestyle isn't easy, but the athletes who are willing to do something hard after school are also more willing to apply themselves in the classroom, in their relationships with family and friends, and as citizens of their community.

Before you evaluate the relative success or failure of the competitive season, ask yourself what sort of citizens you are sending out into the world and how many of them are furthering their education in college. In the big picture, these are the achievements you want to be remembered for.

I was fortunate to guide 14 teams to Washington state championships in boys cross country and had athletes advance to the Foot Locker national finals nine times. But I am no less proud of the fact that 43 of my Mead runners went on to compete in college and that many more attained college degrees and built strong, loving relationships. Satisfaction that comes from a well-oiled program is built on what happens to your athletes after they graduate.

Maintaining relationships with your cross country alums is vital to the overall mission. As your runners graduate and move into college and some of them continue running at the next level, they continue to serve as role models for younger athletes coming up. Additionally, your alumni may move on physically, but emotionally and spiritually they may remain connected to the program. Your grads and their families may continue to be stakeholders in your program. And they are valuable as recruiters, as volunteers, or even as financial supporters.

Season Evaluation

When the season began, you probably stated a few goals that were within reason. Maybe it was a top-five finish at the district championships or a .500 record in league dual meets. Perhaps it was a top-four trophy at the state championships.

At some point after the conclusion of the season, it is worthwhile to take your assistant coaches out to dinner and thank them for their hard work. And while you're at it, you can discuss the relative ups and downs of the season.

Following are questions to ask and discuss with your assistant coaches:

- What went right?
- Did the team buy into the vision we laid out before them in August?
- Did the team peak at the end of the year and perform up to expectations?
- Did the team attain its preseason goals?

Also, make an honest assessment of what went wrong:

- Did a bad attitude corrupt the unity of the team?
- Was the team able to put its best performance together when it counted most?
- Was the season plagued by injuries or illness?
- Were there problems with the management of the dual meet you hosted?
- Did you choose the right hotel to stay in on your overnight trip to a midseason invitational?
- Could you have ordered the uniforms earlier? (Were there too many smalls)?

Examine the flow of the season:

- Did the workouts mix well with the calendar of meets?
- Was your schedule too ambitious?
- Was it too easy?
- Was your team over-raced?

Keep notes during the season about the logistical items that turned out well and also the things that caused problems. You and your assistants will probably agree on most of the answers to the questions just listed. And you can go straight to work addressing any of the issues that need improving next season.

Awards Banquet

On the bus ride home from the state meet or whatever event concluded the season, I was quick to focus on what was next on the horizon. "Tomorrow track and field starts," I'd say, or, "This was a rough draft for Foot Locker,"

or, "Dessert comes next week at BorderClash!" Before we got back to school, my assistants and I looked at the results and scratched out the seniors to get an indication of what next year's team would look like.

My attention also quickly turned to our annual awards banquet. Organizing the banquet requires a lot of work in a short amount of time, but it's all worth it to put on a first-class event for the athletes and their families. First of all, it has to be well planned. Reserve the site early. At Mead, we held the awards the night before Veterans Day because there was no school the next day. That way, we could put a lot of energy into it and everyone had the option of sleeping in the next morning. Be sure to hold the awards banquet before the next sport season begins and attention shifts elsewhere. Pick a date as close as possible to the last competition.

I reserved a large area in the school's cafeteria a year in advance, and I made sure that the date was known to all the staff who worked in that part of the building. That usually guaranteed that the tables were set up with coffee and other items that the school provided.

All through the fall, I kept a binder of material that told the story of the season. It often began with our schedule and team roster, and it included the weekly workout schedules, meet results, travel itineraries, newspaper articles, rankings, and any other scrapbook-type materials that were important to the season. I usually went to the printer the day after the state meet and made copies of these booklets for each member of the team. That gave me a few days' window to get the books ready to hand out. I took a photo of each kid on the team during the season and put each runner's photo on his booklet to personalize it. I organized the stack of books by class, so that I could hand them out as I called up each group. Rule No. 1 in putting on an awards banquet: Never leave a kid out. Everybody goes home with something.

The evening began with a potluck. I told the biggest class (the juniors, for instance) that each of them was responsible for a main dish. The next biggest class brought desserts. The next biggest brought salads.

And the smallest brought beverages, cups, plates, and so on.

The first group invited to eat were family members, followed by seniors, juniors, sophomores, and then freshmen. Meanwhile, I had a slideshow going with photos from the season and mellow, cool music playing in the background. When dinner was finished, I moved to the podium to begin the program. I brought up each class as a group and went through the highlights for each kid. Every kid got his booklet, varsity letter or pin, all-state and all-league certificates, or anything else that was due. And each one also had a moment to hear applause from family and teammates.

Then I went to the special awards, and there were generally a handful of them: Captain awards, Most Valuable Freshman, Most Valuable Sophomore, Most Valuable Junior, Most Valuable Senior, and our Inspirational Award (named for Matt Zweifel).

Sometimes I had a guest speaker, such as Tracy Walters (Gerry Lindgren's coach) or Don Kardong (Olympic marathoner and Spokane resident). Ideally, we'd get it going at 6:00 p.m. and be done by 8:30.

Another thing I did at the awards banquet was appoint captains for the next season. This signified the passing of the baton (or torch) from one set of captains to another. The new captains shadowed the current ones through the winter and spring track season, learning how to lead.

End-of-Year Goal Setting With Athletes

Once you have a team rolling, you know what you have to do. But when you are establishing a team, stated goals are more important. With a new situation, it's important to sit down with the team and discuss what the mission is. Based on what happened the previous year, how high do you set the bar? Perhaps you placed fourth out of eight in the league and everybody is back. You should be in the hunt for the conference title. What's it going to take? Get your runners to believe they're going to do their part. Ask them, "What's your contribution to the team *next* year?"

Goal setting can also happen in one-on-one conferences with the athletes. I might say to a kid, "You were the sixth man last year and two of the guys ahead of you have graduated. Do you see yourself as the No. 4 next fall or No. 1?" This sort of discussion keeps the athlete accountable. What is he or she going to contribute? There are many ways to set goals. Maybe it's as simple as being on

The end-of-season awards banquet is a celebration for a team's hard work. Here, Pat Tyson has a few words to say about Greg Kuntz, a junior who became state champion as a senior in 1989.

time for practice every day. Maybe it's to get a varsity letter. Maybe it's to help the team win the league championship or qualify for state. If they are exceptional athletes, they might have their sights set on a state title or a berth at Foot Locker.

A goal can be to run a specific time, which is discussed in chapter 8. A goal can also be to become a team leader, perhaps a captain, and that would require a thorough discussion about responsibilities and expectations. It's nice to know how your returning athletes see themselves fitting into the next season, and it provides you the opportunity to encourage continued commitment. Reinforce the goal by stating it back: "I like what you are going to contribute to the team. That type of dedication to training could put you right in our mix for a top-seven spot."

One Size Doesn't Fit All

It doesn't matter how talented a runner is, there is a goal out there for everybody. It could be that the goal is to show up every day and run. It could be a personal challenge to lose 15 pounds. That's progress.

I remember a kid who came out for the team at Mead one fall who was overweight. He looked like he belonged on the JV football team's defensive line. The first day he came to practice and began to run, I was standing near him and I felt the ground shake!

He did not look like he was having any fun that first day. But he was determined to lose weight and improve his health, and with the support of his teammates and his own desire and commitment, he stuck with it. By the end of that first season, his body was rapidly transforming. He was still big, but much leaner. Two years later, as a senior, he cracked into our varsity top seven. He lost 75 pounds (34 kg) during his three years at Mead and gained immeasurable confidence. He became a 1:56 800-meter runner.

The bottom line is that there are many ways to win in cross country. You can win by having kids score new personal bests. You can win by helping a kid lose weight and gain self-confidence.

Mead Pyramid

John Wooden, the famous UCLA basketball coach, is one of the coaches I have long admired. His Pyramid of Success is one of the most widely used templates for coaching, business, and life.

When I arrived at Mead, I found that a couple of coaches, Tom Buckner and Gary Baskett, had put together their own pyramid (see figure 13.1). Buckner was the head track and field and cross country coach from 1978 to 1986. Baskett was the head track coach from 1987 to 2000. Between them, they had 15 state track and field team trophies and a record of 186-6 in dual meets. Tom created the pyramid and Gary Baskett passed it on. I inherited it and liked it, and it became one of our traditions. The pyramid is made up of steps for becoming a champion.

Bottom Row

- **Prioritize.** Make training and preparation an important element in your life. You can maintain a home, social, school, and training balance if you prioritize. When you say something is a priority, you are committed to making it a major and important part of your life.

- **Maintain positive self-talk.** More than 90 percent of the words you hear everyday are your own, speaking in your mind to yourself. You are already aware what it feels like when someone puts you down in a cutting, embarrassing, or demeaning way. Why would you do the same thing to yourself? So, speak to yourself positively everyday, all day.

- **Visualize.** This is the powerful partner to positive self talk. When you see yourself perfectly executing a skill in competition, your body internalizes that image. Make your visualization as detailed as possible, including technique, feelings, sounds, and sensations. Your visualizations should be positive, clear, vivid, and successful.

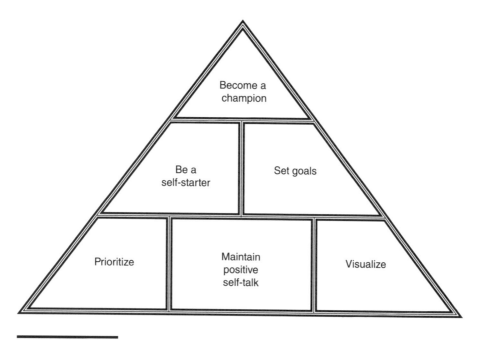

FIGURE 13.1 Mead pyramid.

Middle Row

- **Be a self-starter.** A self-starter doesn't need his mom to get him up for morning training. A self-starter doesn't need to be told by the coach to get after it. The passion and urge to excel comes without constant prodding. Strive to be excitedly self motivated, driven from within, and committed to each aspect of your program.

- **Set goals.** When you have a clear goal, you will get there. Write down your short term, intermediate, and long term goals. They must be what you expect of yourself, what you can realistically achieve with hard work. Post your goals in your bedroom, locker, notebook, and on your refrigerator. Once you've achieved your goals, set new ones!

Top Row

- **Become a champion.** An athlete that is a champion is classy, gracious, confident, strong of spirit, team oriented, willing to serve, humble, happy, mentally tough and right, talented, consistent, and someone you can count on to go the extra mile in sport, friendship,

and family. Memorable, respected champions are great people as well as athletes.

College Recruiting

As a high school coach who is an expert in your athletes' chosen sport, you will often be asked to advocate for your athletes during the college recruiting process.

I'll be honest. Sometimes I was upset with college coaches who went straight to one of my kids without contacting me first. It's like asking permission for marriage: Can I recruit your kid?

Early in my coaching career I tried to stay out of the recruitment process as much as I could, but then I saw athletes fall through the cracks because they weren't well informed and it became apparent that my active role was necessary. My biggest responsibility was to remind athletes of the NCAA's rules and the clearinghouse due dates. That meant taking college placement tests as early as possible so they didn't conflict with the fall cross country season.

I held firm to a team rule: No recruiting trips during the fall season. There was plenty of time after the season was over to take official visits and go through the process of selecting the best fit. That didn't mean that college coaches couldn't come visit us. Coaches made appointments to come by and sit in the library to talk to an athlete and me, or sometimes we talked at the athlete's home with his parents. Some college coaches didn't like my stance on visits. I countered that my athletes could visit them in late December, January, and February. Sometimes it meant being direct with them.

The advice I gave my athletes was consistent: Don't always take the offer with the most money, because you might not be happy. Don't get sucked in by a slick official visit. The college trip is a honeymoon, not the real world. Talk to the athletes. Is the team functional? Is it a family? What do the athletes at that particular school major in?

I suggested that an athlete with a lot of choices pick one dream school, one he could afford, and three in the middle. Then he wrote letters to all five coaches so they knew he was interested. Today, I would emphasize emailing coaches, staying persistent, and taking the college entrance exams more than once.

College athletics is an experience all its own, but it's nothing like those raw, wide-eyed high school years when kids first fell in love with the sport of running.

Summary

The end of the season is the perfect time to reflect on what's going right and what's going wrong with the cross country program. It's important to be able to give an honest assessment of what's happening and pinpoint places where you can improve.

- Evaluate the overall success of your cross country program based on the quality of the people you are helping to mold. Sportsmanship, character, and academic achievement are important measuring sticks for success.

- Assess how the team fared against preseason goals. Did the team meet the goals or fall short? And why?

- Make an honest assessment of what went wrong. Decide in which areas the program has room to grow and improve.

- Make a checklist of questions, and answer them at the end of the season when the details are still fresh in your memory.

- Organize an awards banquet to cap the season and makes each member of the team feel special and valued.

- Meet with runners who will return to the program the following fall and set preliminary goals.

- Take an active role in the college recruitment process so that you can advocate for your kids and help them make informed decisions.

INDEX

Note: The italicized *f, p,* and *t* following page numbers refer to figures, photos, and tables, respectively.

ABOUT THE AUTHORS

Pat Tyson developed his philosophies of training and competition while associating with legendary coaches and runners. He ran at the University of Oregon for Bill Bowerman, the coach of four NCAA champion teams and the cofounder of Nike, Inc. While at Oregon, he was a teammate and roommate of Steve Prefontaine, Olympian and winner of three individual NCAA Men's Cross Country Championships.

Recognized as one of the most successful cross country coaches in the United States, Tyson currently serves as head cross country and track and field coach at Gonzaga University, a position he has held since 2008. Before accepting his position with Gonzaga, Tyson held similar positions at the University of Oregon and University of Kentucky and spent 20 years at Mead High School in Washington while developing it into a distance running powerhouse. During Tyson's time of coaching at Mead, the Panthers achieved an impressive record of 180-8 in one of the toughest dual-meet leagues in the nation. Reaching state competition 18 consecutive years to win 12 state titles, they never placed worse than third. During that time, the Panthers had a nine-year streak when they never lost a competition. In his last three years at Mead, Tyson's teams placed third, fourth, and fifth at the Nike Cross National Championships held in Portland, Oregon.

For his remarkable work with the Mead Panthers, Tyson has been named Washington Coach of the Year multiple times. He was nominated for National High School Coach of the Year when his Mead teams were ranked No. 1 by *Harrier* magazine. Tyson has produced nine Washington prep champions and nine Foot Locker Cross Country Championship finalists. Several of his runners have placed on the All-Time Top 100 List for the state of Washington.

As a competitive athlete, Tyson ran cross country and track at the University of Oregon, where he competed in two NCAA Cross Country Championships and helped lead Oregon to first- and third-place finishes.

Doug Binder is the editor of DyeStat, the internet home of high school cross country and track and field. His professional sports writing career spans 18 years, including 10 as a high school and track and field writer for Portland's *The Oregonian* newspaper, where he has covered numerous running championships at the high school, college, and professional levels. In 2008, Binder led the newspaper's coverage of the Olympic Trials. Before his position at *The Oregonian*, Binder spent three years at the *Gazette-Times* in Corvallis, Oregon, and two at the *Daily Chronicle* in Bozeman, Montana. He is a member of the Track and Field Writers of America.

In 2005, Binder documented Pat Tyson's final days at Mead High School. Those interviews sparked a friendship that endures to this day.